SPIRITUAL JOURNEYS

Michael Connolly began working at the age of fourteen, and throughout his life held a variety of jobs such as factory hand, construction worker and bar person, to name but a few. His interest in writing began in 1979, and since that time he has written a number of poems and experimented with script writing for radio, television and theatre. This is his first book. In more recent years, he has devoted much of his time to researching and experimenting with the hidden powers that lie dormant in the depths of the human psyche.

Spiritual Journeys

Teachings from another dimension

MICHAEL CONNOLLY

ASHFIELD
Press

This book was typeset by
Gough Typesetting Services for
ASHFIELD PRESS,
an imprint of Blackhall Publishing Ltd,
26 Eustace Street. Dublin 2.
(e-mail: blackhall@tinet.ie)

A catalogue record for this book
is available from the British Library

ISBN 1-901658-07-4

Printed by
Betaprint Ltd

Dedications and Acknowledgments

This book is dedicated to my wife, Susan, for her love, patience and understanding. A special thanks, too, for her invaluable assistance in typing and editing this book.

Thanks also to my Guides for their gift of the *Philosopher's Stone*.

Table of Contents

BOOK II

The Teachings

FREEDOM

Freedom is a bird in flight,
Freedom is the wind,
Freedom is inherent, yet
Imprisoned in mankind.

Terrorists and warlords,
They ravage, kill and maim;
Then shout that lack of freedom
Is the fundamental blame.

If man could only realise,
If man could only see,
If each could break the chains *within*,
All mankind would be free.

Michael Connolly

Introduction

Book I, *The Journeys*, is a chronicle of personal "psychic" experiences. These experiences occurred over a period of many years, and are attributed mainly to my research into the subject of parapsychology. Parapsychology, in its broadest sense, examines the lesser known powers that normally lie dormant in the human psyche. These powers include extra-sensory perception (ESP), direct telepathy, psychometry, clairvoyance, clairaudience, prediction, mediumship, channelling and astral projection. Although I investigated, and used, all these innate psychic faculties, it is the latter − astral projection, in particular, that underpins the subject matter of this book.

Astral projection, also known as "remote viewing," "travelling clairvoyance" and "out-of-body experience", is basically, the projection of consciousness beyond the confines of the physical body. In other words, the physical body is left lying inertly, while consciousness travels to other dimensions or planes of existence. These "dimensions" include the earth, etheric, and elemental energy planes but, fundamentally, they are what is traditionally called the "astral planes."

So, what are the astral planes? The Collins, New National Dictionary tells us:

> ". . . in Theosophy, [astral is] the astral sphere connected with our earth and its inhabitants." And, ". . . astral body, a body built of matter of the astral plane, i.e. an octave higher than that of the physical."

The words "matter" and "octave," as they are used in this definition, pertain to a state and frequency of energy respectively. In Cosmic terms, each frequency of energy is determined by its own particular vibration rate, which ranges from relatively dense material energy to very subtle Divine energy. In between these two extremes lie the astral planes.

In essence, then, the astral planes are fields or frequencies of energy of varying degrees of subtlety. Each degree (vibration rate) of subtle energy represents not only a plane, or frequency, of energy, but also exists as a "world" in its own right. By wilfully attuning to these energy frequencies, consciousness can "visit" the astral dimensions, observe their respective landscapes, and converse (telepathically) with their inhabitants. And by the same energy link, the inhabitants of the astral/spirit dimensions can communicate with human consciousness.

Who are the inhabitants of the astral planes? In my experience, the majority of these beings are souls/spirits who once lived on earth. They retain the ego-consciousness and physical appearance of their last incarnation, and carry on their "work" just as they did on earth. Perhaps the most amenable and accessible to human beings are angels and spirit guides. The purpose of these beings is to help people fulfil their respective destinies and, at the same time, raise the collective level of awareness and understanding.

After my first encounters with spirit guides, I found myself in a dilemma: Were the guides "real" entities? Were they figments of an overly fertile imagination? Or, worse still, were they aberrant, autonomous fragments of my own personality?

Over the years, this dilemma dissolved. The more the guides taught me, the more I realised the value of their teachings. Throughout this time, I kept a written record of my meetings with these beings and what they had to say.

To get a clear picture of each subject, many meetings were necessary and many questions had to be asked. For this reason, in Book II, *The Teachings*, the dates of each meeting are omitted to avoid confusion. Also, my Guides' names have been left out at their request. When I asked the reason for this, they explained that if a thousand readers initiated a simultaneous desire to contact, or invoke, them by name, this cumulative desire to make contact would create a "draw" or "pull" on their energy fields. They added, somewhat facetiously, that they wished to remain free spirits, in both name and nature. You will notice, too, that in the Guides' dialogue the first letter of some titles have been capitalised, for example, "Soul/Spirit," "Cosmos," etc. This was also at their request. The reason given was that, whenever possible, it was their wish to give deference to the Higher Order of things.

Finally, throughout this book, when the words "man" and "mankind" are used, they are meant to represent all men and women equally. In the Cosmic scheme of things, all creation is equal. Maybe someday, in our own world, this too shall come to pass.

BOOK I

The Journeys

Meeting an Angel

On a night in March 1979, I had a strange experience. When I say "strange," I mean it was an experience completely foreign to me at that time. Although I did not realise it immediately, this incident had such a profound influence on me that it shaped the rest of my life. It happened during sleep, which, quite naturally, took me completely unawares; there were no preliminaries or forewarnings. At first, I thought my somnolent encounter might have been an extraordinary, vivid dream. But, as I discovered some years later, what occurred that night was much, much more than an extraordinary dream.

I stood in a circular courtyard surrounded by white buildings. My surroundings did not seem to interest or intrigue me, but there was a strong sense of purpose about my being there. I had a distinct feeling that I was waiting for someone to meet me. Furthermore, I felt that this someone had an important message for me. It seemed as if I had been waiting a long time, so much so, that I began to feel impatient. I was aware of a slight "pull" on my entire body, and this contributed to the feeling of impatience. Just as I was about to turn around and search for an exit from the courtyard, a tall being appeared. He was dressed in a white, ankle-length robe. For some reason or other, I construed that the being who stood before me was an angel. Although this thought was foremost in my mind, there was nothing "angelic" about the being. His face was expressionless and I detected an air of formality about him.

He carried a scroll in both hands. Suddenly, while holding on to one end, he let the furled scroll fall to the ground. The scroll rolled past me, unfurling as it went. Then its motion stopped about ten feet away from where I stood. I could see that more than half of the parchment was covered in lines of handwritten text.

The being proffered the portion of the scroll that he held in his hand. I interpreted this gesture as an invitation to read its contents. As I began reading, I noticed that the text was written in a foreign language; yet, I seemed to understand every word. It was not long before I discovered that the scroll contained a written account of my whole life – from beginning to end. As I read through the text, I was astonished by the accuracy and detail of my life history to date. How every single detail of my entire life could fit on a relatively short piece of parchment also intrigued me. But strangest of all was the fact that, in my future life, I was destined to become a writer.

I awoke with a tremendous feeling of euphoria. My first thoughts began

3

to process what I had experienced. Had it been a dream? If it had, then it would have been the most lucid and astounding dream I had ever had. I had a natural tendency to remember my dreams on waking, but, nine times out of ten, the dream memory would fade from consciousness after a short period of time. What took place in my sleep that night was different. Apart from all the written details about my future life, I could remember every other aspect of the dream with a clarity I had never before experienced. Even to this day, almost twenty years later, the memory of this "dream" is as clear as the moment it happened.

At first, it crossed my mind that my experience might have been some form of vision. But, as far as I knew at the time, visions were the privilege of saints and holy people, and I was far from being a saint or holy person. Could the white-robed being in the dream really have been an angel? To my mind, angels only made contact with religious or spiritual people. Again, I was neither religious nor spiritual. Although I had been brought up a Roman Catholic, the rigours of my adult lifestyle displaced any religious leanings I may have had. And my idea of spirituality evoked images of gaunt, white-haired ladies praying in front of statues, in the silence of the daytime Church. Being ignorant of what spiritually was all about, and being a macho man of the first order, I considered all things spiritual to be cissyish.

But there was the question of the scroll and its detailed account of my life. To my perception, the written text had appeared "foreign," and yet it seemed I had known it all my life. I explained this away as being a quirk of the vision-like dream. As for the details of my life history up until that time, well, that was easier to explain. These would have been stored in the subconscious mind.

I then tried to recall details of my future life that I had seen written on the scroll. Although I subconsciously "remembered" most of it on wakening, I could only consciously recall a few of the specific details. The one that struck me most was the fact that writing for a living would feature prominently, at some point in my future life. The prospect of being a writer struck a chord somewhere in the depths of my being. The feeling was akin to a sense of deja-vu: a memory, not from the past, but from the future.

As I lay awake analysing the dream, my rational mind argued that becoming a writer was impossible. I left school before the age of fourteen and, up until 1979, had not considered further education. I could write a basic letter, but that was the extent of my literary capabilities. After leaving school, I had worked at various labouring jobs, and had, more or less, accepted labouring as my lot in life. So, from this standpoint, I felt that becoming a writer was as attainable as becoming a brain surgeon. Considering these limitations, the "angel's" message seemed even more enigmatic.

Had I been familiar with Jungian psychology then, I may have reached a different conclusion about the "angel." I may have decided that the being was simply an archetype – a religious representation of some aspect of my psyche that wanted to express a sublimated, unconscious desire.

Or, had I known what astral projection was like, I would have understood what had taken place. In most dreams conscious awareness flits from one scenario to the next, without rationalising or critically evaluating the content of the dream. However, during a projection of consciousness (astral projection) one has access to sensory faculties, intellectual processes and emotional feelings, just as one would in full waking consciousness. In this state, one can reflect on, and evaluate, ninety per-cent of what takes place. But I did not know this back then. I had an inkling of what astral projection was about, but no idea of what it was like.

In Search of Knowledge

Following my experience in 1979, I developed a thirst for knowledge. Not only did I set about educating myself in the use of the written word, but I also began reading books on parapsychology. Parapsychology deals with the lesser known powers of the human mind; these powers include extra-sensory perception, psychometry, telepathy, telekinesis, clairvoyance, clairaudience, prediction, and remote viewing (astral projection).

In studying these subjects, I realised that there was much more to ourselves and the world around us than met the untrained eye. Not only did I come to this realisation by study, but it was also reinforced by first-hand experiences. For example, one night, shortly after the "dream," I had three visitors. It was chilly in the flat where I lived, and I had an upright, electric heater set in the centre of the living room. This heater stood on four legs – normally, that is. While we were having a cup of tea, suddenly one of the visitors pointed at the heater, and shouted: 'Look!' Some invisible force had tipped the heater onto its back legs; it stood in that position, perfectly balanced, for five to ten seconds. Then, it slowly and smoothly returned to its normal position. Had it not been for the presence of three eyewitnesses, I would have attributed this incident to an hallucination.

In my quest for knowledge it was not surprising that I came across books on the subject of astral projection. One of the first I read was a book called *Astral Doorways*, written by J. H. Brennan. From this book, I learned the principles of astral projection, as well as techniques, "doorways," for projecting consciousness. I also learned, from this book and others, that the out-of-body-experience (astral projection) is not an uncommon phenomenon. It is not something unique to mystics or sorcerers, but is attainable, and indeed practised, by ordinary human beings from all walks of life.

At first, I was smitten by intrigue and a subsequent desire to experience astral projection for myself. But my initial attempts at practising were fraught with unfounded fears. I would ask myself questions like, 'What if I project my astral body to God knows where, and it does not return?' or 'What if my consciousness becomes damaged during this process?' On top of these uncertainties, my earlier endeavours to venture into unknown worlds brought fears of a different nature. After practising the techniques for promoting astral projection a number of times, I began to wake from sleep to find myself in a state of total paralysis. In the course of my research, I learned that this condition is called "cataleptic rigour" and usually accompanies the early stages of learning the art of projection. Many people experience cataleptic rigour during nightmares; it is like being chased by something, or someone, and not being able to move a muscle. Although catalepsy is frightening, it does not endure for long.

However, waking up in this abnormal state was sufficient to inhibit my initial enthusiasm for astral travel, and, consequently, I abandoned the practices. To fill the void in my spare time, I switched my attention to studying the Tarot, crystal-gazing and various forms of divination. These subjects fall into the parapsychology category, and the successful employment of any of these "arts" relies solely on the use of the psychic power, or the "psychic faculty" as I call it. Psychic power is not an external force; it is a latent power inherent in all sentient beings. Generally, psychic activity is a subconscious process, and the effects of its power can only be detected by keen observation. Psychic power, as the name implies, operates from a level of being, known as the "psyche." And, as a matter of interest, the word "psyche" comes from the Greek language and means "of the spirit or soul."

Spontaneous Telepathy

London, England

Between 1980 and 1982, I had a number of successes in psychic matters. These successes proved to me, beyond any doubt, the efficacy and validity of psychic power. Not only that, but the experiences I encountered in the early stages lured me into a further fifteen years of experimenting with, and researching, the powers of the human psyche.

My first experience demonstrated to me the reality of telepathy. In the run-up to this particular event, I had been meditating regularly – fifteen to twenty minutes, both morning and night. Each evening, after work, I also set aside time for the practice of crystal gazing; a practice that was new to me at the time.

One evening, during the long car journey home from work, one of my co-workers initiated a card guessing game. He sat in the front passenger seat; I and two other colleagues sat in the back. The fellow in front selected a card from a pack of playing cards, and, keeping it below the level of his seat, he asked if we could guess which card he held. Bets were made, and whoever guessed the card correctly won the "pot." To cut a long story short, I had seven correct guesses in succession. Each time a card was pulled from the pack, I saw the image of the card in my mind's eye. After that, the card guessing game degenerated into a debate about my achievement. One said it was "luck"; another suggested that I had somehow used the car mirrors to view the selected cards. Both of these suggestions were wrong, and not even I could offer a definitive explanation.

Later that evening, when I had time to reflect fully, it dawned on me that what had happened in the car was a case of telepathy, pure and simple. But, what had triggered, or activated, this ability? At the time I had no idea.

The Past-Life Dream

My next experience opened a pathway that led me to believe in reincarnation. I awoke around 3a.m. one morning and quickly jotted down details from a dream I had been having. In the dream, I was on the deck of an old ship that seemed to be making its way through heavy fog. Suddenly, the ship halted, as if it had run into something solid. As a result of the unexpected stop, I was flung forward. There was some object, about waist high, fixed to the deck of the ship and, as I was propelled headlong, my hip struck this object. I got a distinct feeling that it was made of metal. The impact of my hip striking the object was extremely painful, and it was this pain that woke me up. In the dream, I seemed to "know" that the year was 1894, and that the ship's name was the Taldora. I also felt that I had known the Taldora all my life. Even after I woke up, I still retained a pronounced feeling of kinship, or affinity, with the ship. It was as if I belonged in that time-frame – not in 1981, but in 1894.

After I wrote down the year and name of the ship, I felt a soreness in the bone of my left hip, the one that had been injured in the dream. When I examined the area, I found that there was a redness on the hip bone and it was extremely tender to the touch. Nevertheless, I put it from my mind and went back to sleep.

The next morning my recollection of the dream was still vivid. Again, I felt that this dream was not an ordinary, run-of-the-mill dream. The feeling attached to the dream memory stirred something deep within me. I felt that I knew the ship and that I really had been on the deck when it had come to a sudden halt. This profound sensation seduced me into taking the day off work in order to research the existence, or non-existence, of my "dream ship," the Taldora. I felt that this ship had existed, but I also felt that it was necessary to prove it to myself. It occurred to me that perhaps there might be a record of this ship in Lloyds, one of the largest marine insurance companies at the time.

Later that day, I sat at a desk in one of Lloyds' offices. Before me lay a stack of file-folders, all of them containing information about a ship called the Taldora.

To this day, I regret not having taken as many notes as possible, but amidst the excitement of "finding" the Taldora, and proving to myself that there actually was such a ship, the idea of copying details seemed inconsequential. I had already found what I was looking for: proof of the ship's existence.

It was sixteen years ago since I saw those files, and my memory of the details may not be as accurate as I would like them to be. As far as I can remember, the ship was built in Brisbane in the 1800s. In or around 1894, it is on record that this ship did hit a sandbank during a heavy fog and, consequently, sustained some minor damage. Because the ship was travelling too

fast in foggy conditions, the captain was charged with negligence, and repri-
manded accordingly. I remember these points in particular because of their
relevance to the dream: number one, the existence of the ship in the time-
frame of the dream (1894); and number two, the striking of the sandbank in
foggy conditions. My thanks to the staff at Lloyds for allowing access to this
information.

Some who read this account may say that the content of my dream was
not an authentic past-life memory, but could have been a subconscious recollection of something I had read or seen on television regarding the Taldora. In
my view, my profound feeling of affinity with the ship, both in and immediately after the dream, goes way beyond anything I might have read or seen on
the subject.

Spontaneous Clairvoyance/Clairaudience

My next experience involved both clairvoyance and clairaudience. I was at a friend's house one night around Christmas time. While having a drink with my friend and his wife, the couple from next door arrived and joined us. The only light in the living room came from a table lamp, leaving the room dimly lit. Everyone was relaxed and conversation flowed freely. At one point, I turned my head to address the lady from next door, but was startled into silence by what I saw. Suspended in the air above her head was a large image of a human heart with a sword piercing its centre. At the moment I saw the image, a voice inside my head "said": 'In thine own heart a sword shall pierce.' Then the image faded.

This incident left me quite shaken; so much so, that I found it difficult to concentrate on the ensuing exchanges of conversation. I experienced a dreadful sense of unease, a feeling of foreboding, and this became so overwhelming that I excused myself and left. Outside the house the feeling faded, but as I walked home I was still bewildered by the whole event. What had happened to me? Was it an hallucination? Was I suffering from some form of mental aberration? Some months beforehand, while working in a deep trench on a building site, a fair-sized lump of concrete had fallen on my head, resulting in numerous stitches to the head wound and a seven day headache for good measure. As I thought more and more about the bizarre incident I had just experienced, I naively began to wonder if my brain had been damaged.

Two days later I had forgotten all about the woman, the vision, and the message associated with her. Then, I heard the news that her only son, a young man in his early twenties, had committed suicide that day. At that moment, the significance of the clairvoyant vision and clairaudient voice became apparent. Although I had never met the young man, for reasons unknown, my psychic faculties had acted spontaneously in an attempt to deliver a forewarning.

These experiences copperfastened my interest in parapsychology. But I did not advance in this field as quickly as I would have liked. It seemed that destiny had other plans.

Practising Astral Projection

October 1985 (Dublin, Ireland)

One day, my wife, Susan, who is also an avid reader, came across a book called *Journeys Out Of The Body* by Robert A. Monroe. In this book, Mr. Monroe gives a detailed account of his own experiences of out-of-body travel over a period of ten years. He tells of his ability to detach his "Second Body" (astral body) from the physical. He also relates how he consciously journeyed in this "Second Body" to different dimensions of time and space. Because of the difference in topography of these dimensions, the author classifies them as Locale I, Locale II and Locale III.

Reading about these dimensions and their indigenous inhabitants fired my enthusiasm for astral travel, yet again. And so, without further reservations, I hurled myself full force into these practices. The technique I used involved a number of steps. First of all, I physically carried out a tour of the room where I practised, memorising every detail of the room and all its contents. Next, I lay on the bed and relaxed deeply until a state of drowsiness was reached. I then visualised myself getting up out of bed, as I would physically, and, using my inner vision, "moved" around the room, "looking" at all its details and items, as I remembered them. Most importantly, at the end, I visualised myself "returning" to my physical body. I practised this technique for about an hour each day, keeping it up relentlessly for a number of weeks. Nothing happened until...

The Astral Temple

I lay in bed, mentally performing the same visualising methods that I had been practising. Again nothing happened, so I eventually drifted off to sleep.

A short time after going to sleep, I "awoke" in a state of cataleptic rigour. I had a feeling of movement, but not physical movement; it felt as if some part of me was being involuntarily pulled by an ineffable force. At the same time, it seemed like I was trying to stop the movement – trying to resist it. But I could not. My whole body, from head to toe, felt paralysed. This feeling was so profoundly disturbing that I panicked and struggled desperately to escape from its grip. A voice from somewhere within my being exhorted me to let go, to stop struggling; and following that, an understanding came to me that if I gave up struggling all would be well. Although it was quite a difficult thing to do, I did stop struggling; I stopped trying to wake up.

Then, I did wake up. Though not where I had gone to sleep. I found myself standing in a square, on the outskirts of a city in broad daylight. The square appeared to be constructed of white marble. From where I stood, I could see that the main square enclosed a smaller one; it had three marble steps around its perimeter, leading down into it. To my right, I could see a large water fountain, and on the skyline beyond, groups of buildings were clearly visible. Some of these looked like low, white apartment blocks. The fountain was also of white marble and resembled a chalice in shape. Water spouted upwards from its centre, filled the fountain, then cascaded from its edges into a sparkling pool below. A square duct drew the excess water from the pool and directed it into a stream that lay behind me. This stream was spanned by a marble bridge, which was situated behind me to the left. I "sensed" that this bridge was an entrance to the city. In front and to my left, an area of trees and shrubs ran off into the distance. In the foreground of this area, sat three chalice-shaped, white-marble containers, equally spaced along the edge of the outer square. These containers held growing plants that appeared to be yucca.

Wandering around the square were perhaps half-a-dozen beings identically dressed in white, ankle-length robes. At least two of these beings were female. They strolled casually around the square, some in a clockwise direction, others in an anticlockwise direction. Their faces carried sombre expressions, as if they were engaged in serious contemplation, and although two of them passed within a few feet of where I stood, no one paid any attention to my presence. It was as if I were invisible.

At the thought of being invisible, I directed my attention towards myself. Looking down at my body, I was surprised to see that I, too, was dressed in a white, ankle-length robe. When I examined my arms, I saw that the sleeves of the robe were wide and reached mid-forearm.

Beyond the left-hand corner of the main square, I noticed a large, domed, white building. A number of steps led up to its white, arched door. For some particular reason the building fascinated me, and this evoked a desire to see what was inside. As my thoughts echoed this desire, I found myself standing at the bottom of the steps leading up to the building. I stood there, trying to rationalise how I could have traversed a distance of about three hundred yards and not have any recollection of it. A voice inside my head said: 'Action follows thought.'

I do not remember going up the steps of the building, but the next thing I recall is standing at the white, arched door. To the left of the door, I saw a gold, or brass, plate with letters inscribed on it. My thoughts were sluggish, so much so, that I had to concentrate intently in order to read the inscription. Focussing on the plate, I could see that it read: "God is within." This gave me the impression that the building was some kind of temple. My rational mind pondered the inscribed words: Did they mean that God was within the temple? Or did they imply that God was within myself?

These thoughts seemed to project me into the temple. Again, I had no recollection of movement, and my next awareness was that of standing inside the large, circular building. My mind was still in the process of trying to figure out what the inscription on the plate outside really meant. I felt as if I were both inside and outside the temple, at the same time. Outside, I was looking at the inscribed plate while my conscious mind tried to decipher its meaning; inside, I was now face-to-face with an aged, white-haired man who wore a white robe covered with a red cloak trimmed with gold embroidery.

It became apparent that this sagacious looking man, or being, who stood before me, had access to my thoughts. And as my mind struggled with the question of whether God was within the temple or within myself, he said, 'What do you think?' I told him I had not yet made up my mind, and that, most likely, the inscription meant that God was perhaps in the temple. 'Wrong,' he answered. 'God is within all, and all is within God.'

Now, my mind approached the task of rationalising what the man had just said. He turned, as if he were about to walk away, and, as he did so, he added something about God and electromagnetic energy. I asked him to repeat or explain what he had said. He turned again and looked directly at me. His gaze was penetrating and, for the first time, I noticed that his eyes were azure blue. He said, 'It is too early. You will not understand. Talk about something else.'

My thoughts turned to the aged man. I felt a peculiar curiosity about who he was and, simultaneously, I wondered why I was communicating with him. These thoughts and his response overlapped.

'I am a Guide,' he said. 'We are also called Teachers, Helpers, or Masters. Our titles are irrelevant. It is what we do that is important.'

'What do you do?' I asked.

'We guide the spirit from darkness into light.'

When he mentioned "spirit," I wondered if he were talking about the spirits of dead people.

Again he read my thoughts. 'No. There is no such thing as dead people. The spirit of life never dies: it only changes form.

'We administer to spirits who inhabit bodies of matter [physical bodies]. Our principal task is to provide the stepping stones that lead into light.'

'What do you mean by light?' I enquired.

'Light is wisdom and understanding. Wisdom and understanding set the spirit free. Darkness is ignorance. Ignorance enslaves the spirit in vexations, yearnings, frustrations and endless torment.'

I got the feeling that the Guide's answer was aimed directly at me, personally. At that point in time, I considered myself neither wise nor ignorant. However, the Guide held a different opinion.

'You are trapped in a state of self-perpetuated darkness,' he said. 'You cannot see where the light lies. You do not know where to look. We will guide you.'

At that moment, I had a feeling of being terribly tired. As a matter of fact, I wanted to lie down on the spot where I stood.

The Guide said, 'When you return, we will show you the way.'

My thought processes engaged in pondering what he meant by "the way." Just then, I was aware of myself both lying in bed and standing in the temple. This impression lasted only an instant. My conscious awareness was brought fully back to my physical body by a sensation of a cold wind blowing across my face. In my half-asleep, half-awake state, I attributed the wind to an open bedroom window. The decision to get up and close the window woke me completely. Although I no longer felt the wind, I got out of bed and went to close the window – it was, however, tightly shut.

I stayed up for over an hour assimilating the contents of the whole experience. I felt elated, energetic and wide awake. Something profound had taken place; that much I accepted. Was it, perhaps, a "real" astral projection? I concluded that what I had experienced was, indeed, a projection of consciousness into some other dimension. And if this were a projection, then so too must be my own so-called "extraordinary dream" of 1979. The spirit beings that featured in both episodes were similarly dressed. There was also a similarity between the locations in both instances: each location possessed the same inexplicable quality, or aura.

On a number of occasions between November 1985 and July 1986, I tried to revisit the dimension of the "Marble City." Perhaps I was trying too hard; my attempts were unsuccessful. During that period, I practised meditation twice a day, morning and night, at least four or five days a week. These mediation sessions lasted anywhere from twenty minutes to an hour. In conjunction with some of these sessions, I also practised the visualisation technique for facilitating out-of-body travel.

The Law of Karma

I awoke from sleep, uncomfortably bathed in perspiration, conscious of the fact that I had been dreaming. In the dream, I had been pushing a motor cycle along a crowded street, against the flow of pedestrian and vehicular traffic. While thinking about the dream, I turned on my side and went back to sleep again.

Almost immediately, or so it seemed, I slipped into another "dream." I was once again standing in the same temple that I had "visited" in November of the previous year. I remember being surprised at first, and wondered what how I got there. From somewhere behind me a voice answered, 'You want to know about Karma.' At the sound of the voice, I turned to see who had addressed me, and found myself looking at an aged man. He sat at a rectangular wooden table, in a small alcove off the main floor of the temple, about thirty-five feet from where I stood. A soft, green-yellow light permeated the alcove; it appeared to emanate from the walls.

He beckoned me to him, and just as the thought of moving entered my mind, I was standing by the side of the table, opposite the grey-haired, white-robed man. I had crossed the distance that separated us without being aware of movement. It came to mind that he was not the same being whom I had met on the first occasion. He seemed to be aware of my thoughts and introduced himself by name. He told me that he, also, was a Guide, a Teacher; he said that he had come to meet me because I had wanted to know about Karma – the Universal Law of cause and effect.

Strangely enough, this was the case. Around that period of time, I had been reading a book in which the subject of Karma was briefly discussed. I did want to know more, and I may have been thinking about this subject before going to sleep that night.

'Let us begin,' he said, pointing to a balance (scales) that stood on the table before him. It reminded me of the "scales of justice." It was made of brass. The cross arm and suspended pans were supported by a fluted upright rod about a foot high. The entire apparatus was mounted on a circular, tiered base. In looking at the scales, I understood that it was to be used to illustrate a point, or points, in the lesson about to be conveyed. The Guide held out a closed fist. When he opened it, I saw that it contained a smooth, greyish pebble. He looked directly at me, as if checking to see if I were paying attention. Obviously satisfied, he proceeded with his demonstration. He carefully placed the pebble in the centre of one of the pans. Immediately, that side of the scales dropped, until the pan rested on the table.

'What has happened?' he asked, looking at me quizzically.

'The weight of the pebble has caused one side of the scales to drop,' I answered.

'Yes,' he said. 'That is the action. The pebble did cause one side of the scales to drop. And your eyes were drawn to observe this action. You must bear in mind...'

He pointed to the tray containing the pebble.

'. . . that the drop on this side of the scales caused the other side to ascend.'

He indicated the elevated portion of the scales. 'This is the reaction. This is the effect. For every action there is a proportional reaction. Every cause has an effect.'

I asked him if this law applied to each and every action committed by individual human beings.

'Yes. But your conscious awareness is not developed sufficiently to notice. You [human beings], especially in the commercial world, have developed an unfortunate habit of focussing all your attention on the action you are involved in. While you are doing this you remain blissfully unaware of the reaction to your action. You set something in motion, you cause something to happen; yet you ignore, or deny, responsibility for the effect you have caused.'

I did not quite comprehend what the Guide was getting at. He picked up on my thoughts and went on to elucidate.

'Take drinking habits, for example. On week-ends you go out among other people to socialise. In the process of this so-called socialising you drink more alcohol than is good for you. That is an action. What is the reaction?'

I told him that the effect, or reaction, of a night's drinking was most likely to be a hangover.

'And more,' he exhorted. 'Buying, and consuming, alcohol is an unnecessary and unhealthy waste of money and time. It is not constructive. But you do not notice this. You do not notice or acknowledge these negative reactions to your actions.'

Standing there before the Guide's penetrating gaze made me feel uncomfortable.

'What am I supposed to do?' I asked, fearing that he might advise me to totally renounce my social life.

'Self-observation,' he replied. 'Observe and monitor every action that you habitually carry out. Remember, it is the *habitual* negative actions that wreak the most damage. Watch them. Keep watching until you can pinpoint and evaluate the reaction(s) to your action(s). See how the reaction is affecting you spiritually, mentally, emotionally, physically and financially.'

From somewhere underneath the table, the Guide produced a page about A4 in size, and turned it on its side (landscape view). He thrust the page towards me so that I could see it clearly. There were five vertical lines drawn down the page, dividing it into six columns. The first column was headed *Thought*; the second, *Emotion*; the third, *Action*; the fourth, *Reaction*; the fifth,

Positive; and the sixth, *Negative*. These headings were written in a font style similar to "Script."

'Observe your thoughts, feelings and actions,' the Guide said sternly. 'Keep a daily record; not just of physical actions, but of thoughts and feelings as well. Preceding every action there is always a thought, and most times an emotion. Bear in mind that, as initiators, both thought and feeling are interchangeable and interactive. Sometimes a feeling will initiate a thought or train of thoughts. At other times, thought will trigger an emotion. Regardless of which comes first, there can be no conscious physical action, or reaction, without the presence of thought, emotion, or both. It is, therefore, as important to monitor your thoughts and feelings, as it is to monitor your actions and reactions. Even in instances where no action follows, logging your thoughts and feelings will show if they are predominantly positive or negative. This exercise will help pinpoint negative patterns of thinking and feeling, thereby making way for their elimination, if you so wish.

'By observing your thoughts and feelings, you will begin to understand the workings of the mind and your attitude towards life. By observing your actions, and the reactions to those actions, you will discover how your own state of consciousness is affecting your life. If you carry out this method of self-observation regularly, without fail, your conscious awareness will expand. You will also find out if you are in control of your consciousness – or if your consciousness is in control of you.

'Work on this. Then come back and see me.'

I had no memory of leaving the temple. When I awoke, daylight was filtering through the bedroom curtains. I felt wide awake and charged with energy.

For a period of time I followed the Guide's advice. But despite the efficacy of the self-observation method, my initial determination to keep a log of my daily thoughts, feelings and actions soon declined. An indifference towards self-improvement set in, and my life once again became immersed in the mundane world. Maybe I did not want to change; maybe I was not yet ready for it.

Regardless of the reasons, it was January of the following year before I managed to return to astral travel. I had made a New Year's resolution to the effect that, in the year ahead, I would devote all my free time towards spiritual advancement. Although this did not happen as planned, I did, however, have a number of experiences during 1987.

The Story of the Three Streams

13 January 1987

From the first of January 1987, I applied myself to the practice of meditation and astral projection techniques.

In the middle of practising the astral projection technique, I reached an altered state of consciousness; that is, I had no awareness of my surroundings or my physical body. Suddenly, I felt a lifting, or what could be described as a sense of floating: a distinct feeling of upward movement. In front of and close to my face, I heard four loud clicks in rapid succession. Almost immediately, I heard an even louder bang at the back of my head; it sounded like a rifle shot. At that moment, I was conscious of my body lying in bed, unable to move. Perhaps I had tried to move my physical body following the sound of the shot; hence, my awareness of being in a state of cataleptic rigour.

Without any further physical sensations, I was standing, once again, in the now familiar temple. This time I was greeted by a portly, avuncular character with long, grey hair, wearing ankle-length, red robes that appeared to be made from a velvety material. He enthusiastically thrust out his hand in a gesture eliciting a handshake. I shook his hand. He did not give a name, but simply introduced himself as a Guide.

'Welcome back,' he said.

The words sounded so sincere that I felt guilty, and I began to explain why I had not made the effort to visit for so long. The Guide held up his hand, indicating that there was no need for, or that he did not want to hear, explanations. Without pause he launched himself into the following soliloquy.

'The forward motion of an individual's life should be like that of an abundant stream, flowing clearly and gracefully. All streams flow from a source, and each stream, in order to survive, must have unhindered contact with its own source [contact with Spirit]. As the stream travels its course, it is nourished by tributaries and rivulets [experiences and knowledge] along the way.

'If the stream is enriched by many tributaries and rivulets along its course, it will become wide and deep. It is then that its surface grows calm and still, while its great strength remains active beneath the surface. And when its surface achieves this calm state, the stream becomes like a mirror: a mirror in which heaven and earth can be perceived.

'On the other hand, a stream whose tributaries and rivulets are weak, or non-existent, will remain a narrow, shallow channel, gushing and babbling discordantly along the stones. When a stream is in this condition, neither heaven nor earth can be perceived. Yet, it will still reach its destination.

'If a stream's contact with its source becomes partially hindered or diverted, the stream will become weak. When a stream is weakened in this manner, in times of adversity [dry weather] the stream will cease to be, leaving behind it stagnant pools as evidence of its being.'

At that point, I felt myself being pulled. There was a sound of a fire engine siren; this seemed to be passing the house where I lived. For a fleeting moment, I experienced an awareness of simultaneously lying in bed and leaving the temple. My next awareness was that of being unable to move – every muscle in my body was paralysed. After what seemed like an eternity of struggling, I regained control of my tongue and voice but the rest of my body was still paralysed. I knew, from past experience, that the only way to break out of this deadlock was to be shaken vigorously. Shouting to my wife to "wake" me, she quickly awoke and shook me; it was this movement that extricated me from the inexorable grip of catalepsy.

When I became fully awake and the terror of catalepsy had subsided, I vowed to myself that I would abandon the practice of astral projection forever. With that in mind, I eventually fell asleep.

The following morning, upon awakening, I "heard" a voice coming from somewhere within me. It said: 'Be like an abundant stream. Forward, forward, forever forward; examining each day and each way. Onwards, onwards, forever onwards. That is the flow of life.'

From January until November 1987, I lived up to my vow and abandoned practising astral projection. In a way, it was just as well; during these months my job demanded twelve to fourteen hours a day, which would not have left much time for the contemplation of mystical or spiritual matters.

However, a job change in October brought with it a change of lifestyle. I was left with more spare time on my hands, and soon an undeniable prompt, from some deeper level of my being, compelled me to recommence the practices. Although I still remained fearful of the cataleptic state, my fear had been allayed somewhat. I had read a book in which the author said that the state of catalepsy was something experienced only in the early days of projection, and that this frightening condition would, in time, diminish and ultimately cease.

Spurred on by this promising piece of information, in November 1987, I started practising astral projection again.

Out-Of-Body on the Earth Plane

22 November 1987

During practice, nothing unusual happened until the night of the twenty-second. I lay in bed after practising, drowsy and intending to go asleep. Thoughts drifted through my relaxed mind until, suddenly, I remembered that I had promised to phone a particular person that evening, but had forgotten to make the call. Then and there, I made a mental note to phone the person first thing the following morning.

With that thought firmly in mind, I can only assume that I fell asleep. Without any preliminary sensation of movement, psychic noise or cataleptic rigour, I found myself outside the bedroom and in the hallway, standing in front of the telephone. My conscious mind seemed bent on making the phone call as planned; even to the point where an image of the person I intended to call flashed into my mind. I reached out to lift the telephone receiver with my left hand, while my right hand reached out to dial the number. Confusion followed. I saw that my left hand had passed through the entire telephone. My rational mind could not comprehend what was happening: it was not used to seeing my hand pass through solid objects, and as far as it was concerned, I was standing in the hallway in my corporeal body. I experienced a numbness in my mind. It was like being highly intoxicated and not being able to coherently formulate thoughts. I then tried lifting the receiver with my right hand, but that too passed through the telephone. When I tried dialling, the same thing happened.

Perhaps if my rational mind had realised that my consciousness now inhabited a non-material body, it would have been easier to come to terms, and experiment with, this new-found mode of getting around. But it did not. Instead, my mind rationalised that there was something wrong with the telephone; that it was out of order, simply because I was unable to use it. The thought struck me that I should go to the phone box at the end of the street, make the call I had to make, and, while there, report my own phone out of order.

Just as that train of thought settled in my mind, I found myself in the phone box at the end of the street. Again, there was no sensation of movement. The instant I formulated the intention of using the phone box a quarter of a mile away, I arrived there, inside it. I had travelled to the phone box at the "speed of thought."

But, not surprisingly, when I tried to use the public phone, I encountered the same difficulty as I did with my own: my hands kept passing through it.

After a few futile attempts to use the phone, the notion occurred to me that I should give up and go home.

Instantaneously, I was there. I stood in the semi-darkness of the bedroom, by the side of the bed that I sleep on, looking at two dim figures tucked underneath the covers. The light was too poor to distinguish the features of either of the two heads on the pillows. My logical mind searched for a reason as to why some person occupied my place in bed. But my consciousness was still hazy. I tried to remember if we had had a visitor that evening; if we had perhaps invited the visitor to stay overnight; and if so, what was he or she doing in my bed. I decided that whoever it was would have to leave. I began pulling at the body in bed, but, strangely, I could not find a grip. Even stranger was the fact that the body in bed began to pull at me. When I felt myself (my astral body) being pulled by this "stranger," I panicked and resisted the pull. At that point, I felt a fleeting awareness of simultaneously lying down and standing up. The stranger in bed was my physical body: the one standing up beside the bed was my astral body. Consciousness momentarily split between the two "vehicles." I could feel my physical body, in its paralysed state, struggling to pull the astral body back into its normal habitat; at the same time, I was conscious of my astral body being pulled by the physical.

Within a number of seconds, I awoke, with all my faculties intact and with a clear, detailed memory of the entire experience.

The Spirit Healers

Night-time, during sleep, I became conscious of myself walking along a corridor. There was something clinical about it, but I could not figure out what it was. A bright, pale green light filled the corridor, yet the light had no visible source. It seemed to shine through, or emanate from, the walls.

Suddenly, I realised why I sensed the clinical quality about the place: the corridor, where I stood, had the distinctive ambience of a hospital. I felt an urge to explore and, just as I was about to move, I felt myself being pulled towards, and into, a medium-sized, rectangular room. The room had two doors but no windows. Centred by one wall was a metal-framed, single bed with white pillows, sheets and bed-cover. On the right-hand side of the bed stood a brown, wooden, bedside locker. Like the corridor where I had been, the room seemed to be part of a hospital, and looked like any modern, private ward, but without the mod cons.

I sensed that I had come to this place for a reason; it was as if I knew the reason but could not remember. I struggled hard to recollect, but discovered that thinking drained my energy. A feeling of tiredness followed, and I thought that lying in the vacant bed would revive me.

As I stretched out on the bed, I noticed that I wore a white robe with three-quarter length sleeves. Lying there on the bed, in what I construed to be a hospital, made me think of healing. In a way, the tiredness I experienced bordered on the feeling of enervation usually associated with illness.

At that point, the door to my left opened and two middle-aged, male beings entered the room. They were dressed in white robes similar to my own. They both came over, stood by the left-hand side of the bed, and gazed at me with expressionless faces. Although their looks were far from friendly, I sensed no animosity or threat. It seemed as if they had come to carry out some task, and that the expedition of this task was all that interested both of them. The being closest to me, who was the taller of the two, produced a large, black, hardback book from behind his back, and handed it to me. As I took the book, I noticed that it had *The Bible* inscribed in gold lettering on the front cover. When the book was in my hands, it fell open to a page which revealed a picture of myself at that moment. The picture showed me lying on the white-covered bed, in my white robe, propped up by pillows and holding a black covered book. The caption underneath the picture read: "Spiritual Healing".

I looked at the being closest to me. 'What is spiritual healing?' I asked.

'I will show you,' he said. With that, he reached out and took my wrist.

The effect of his action was indescribable. Successive bands of electrical energy swept up and down my body. There were hundreds of these energy bands; they felt like cinctures rolling along my body's surface. I discovered that I could focus my attention on individual bands as they travelled from the top of my head to my feet. At the same time, I was aware of all the successive energy bands moving upwards and downwards, concurrently.

The experience was so shocking that I shortly woke up. And as I awoke, I could still feel the surges of electrical energy running up and down my physical body. Although now the feeling was not totally unpleasant, it was uncomfortable. Not having had this experience before, I was somewhat frightened by it, and, in an attempt to stop what was happening, I leaped out of bed and headed for the living room. By the time I reached the living room, the energy surges had given way to an intense tingling all over my body. I drank tea and smoked a couple of cigarettes, trying to bring myself back to normal. Over a period of twenty minutes, much to my relief, the tingling diminished and finally ceased.

Even though this experience had, once again, left me apprehensive about the whole business of astral travel, I managed to make few half-hearted attempts during January 1988.

The Cosmic Diagram

From sleep, I became aware of myself climbing something that looked like a sheer wall of earth which was covered with abundant growth: young saplings, small bushes and coarse grass. I pulled myself along using this vegetation as hand-holds. Fear made me cling to each hold tightly. I felt that I was at a great height, and that below, a fatal drop awaited me should any of my hand-holds give way. The fear which I experienced seemed real; I felt it in the region of my solar plexus. Suddenly, a pair of sandaled feet loomed in front of me. Tilting my head back as far as I could to identify the owner of the feet, I saw, standing over me, the figure of a woman dressed in russet robes. From my position, it seemed as if she were standing out from, and at a right-angle to the wall of earth. Confusion set in. I could not figure out how this woman could anchor herself at such an angle above a drop of thousands of feet. 'It all depends on the way you look at it,' she said. Up until then, because of my fear, I had not dared to look down, but the reassurance in the woman's voice urged me to take stock of my own position. After looking around me, I realised that I was not climbing a sheer wall after all; I was pulling myself along flat ground.

At that point, the fear of falling disappeared and, almost immediately, it was replaced by thoughts of what I had been searching for in the first instance. I had been trying to make my way somewhere. "Home" came to mind. I asked the woman which way I should go. She did not answer verbally, but pointed off into the distance. There was a red sun setting on the horizon and this is what she appeared to be pointing at.

I set off in the direction of the sun, not walking or running, but gliding horizontally, with my body about four to six feet off the ground. I could clearly see the terrain beneath fly past my field of vision.

Suddenly, there was a bang, like an explosion. Not only did I hear the noise, but I also felt it as a reverberation throughout my whole being. Seemingly, I had struck some kind of barrier, which on examination appeared to be both fluid and solid. It looked like a wall of white, marbled vapour. I got the feeling that I could pass through it, yet I also felt that if I tried, it would repel me and cause another explosion. It occurred to me that I would eventually have to pass through this mystifying substance in order to get home. As I cogitated my situation, a tall, long-haired man dressed in a white robe stepped out from the wall of white vapour.

'What are you looking for?' he demanded.

I told him that the wall was separating me from my home.

'There is no separation in the Cosmos,' he answered. 'Everything is one.'

With that, he held out his left hand, palm upwards, for me to see. It flashed into my mind that what he was showing me was a diagram of the Cosmos.

The diagram looked like a circular, spider's web, radiating outwards from a central point. Each strand, each filament, in the web was alive and pulsating with tiny atoms or sparks of light. These tiny lights issued from the central point and undulated all the way along the entire length of the strands as far as the outer limits; then, in the same graceful, undulating manner, they returned to the source. There were millions of them, going out and coming in at the same time. It was a fascinating sight and captured my full attention, until the being's voice distracted me.

'You can't go through there,' he said, pointing to the vapour-like wall.

'Why not?' I asked.

'It's electric. It will give you a shock,' he answered. He then showed me the palm of his right hand; it held a picture of the street where I lived. As I looked at the picture, it gradually became larger until it engulfed me. I had two sensations: one of being pulled towards the street; the other of being swallowed by the whole scene in the picture.

At that point, I awoke, safely back in my physical body.

Attacked by a Ghost

This time, while lying in bed before sleep, I was consciously trying to lift out of my body. My intention was to take a trip around the neighbourhood using the astral vehicle.

Before long, I was hovering horizontally, in a supine position, about three feet above my physical body. Suddenly, the form of a stout, dark-haired woman descended from the ceiling. She held a shiny skewer in both hands, and, before I realised what was happening, she plunged the skewer through my throat.

I felt a sharp, intense pain accompanied by a sensation of choking. Both these impressions carried over into my physical body which had now become wide-awake and fully conscious from the shock of what had happened. The sense of choking was extreme; it felt as if some viscous material clogged my whole throat, blocking the air passages in the process. Coughing and spluttering, I jumped up and sat on the edge of the bed. The coughing spasms, stinging pain and the feeling of mucous blocking my throat – all lasted for more than ten minutes. After these symptoms had passed, I was still left with a stinging soreness in the throat. The effects of this bizarre incident were frequently repeated for about a year afterwards. Not by visitations from my ghostly, female adversary, but, on numerous nights, I awoke with the same choking sensation and stinging pain in the throat.

Not surprisingly, after this particular episode, I once again ceased the practice and research of all things psychic.

Years later, I asked my Guides about the woman who attacked me. They said she was an earthbound spirit of a woman who had lived in that house before it had been converted into flats. The woman was, and always had been, possessive about her house; it had been her pride and joy. Now, she resented other people living there, and, whenever she got the opportunity, she vented that resentment. She could not successfully attack physical bodies, but, when my energy body emerged that night, she availed of the chance to assault me. I asked the Guides why she had not attacked me on other occasions when I was out-of-body. The Guides said I was lucky – the woman had not been in the house at those times.

Literary Endeavours

Throughout 1988, my interest in writing deepened. I read books on all aspects of writing, in the hope of discovering what kind of writer I was destined to become. Was it journalist, poet, short story writer, scriptwriter, playwright or novelist? I had no idea where to begin.

Shortly after the revelation, in 1979, regarding my future career as a writer, I had started to write lyrical poetry. By 1988, I had written more than twenty poems and a few children's stories, but came to realise that the market for this kind of material is limited. And so, I ambitiously pitched my writing endeavours into other areas.

Over a twelve month period, I wrote a few pilot script proposals for television situation comedy programs, a radio play and a full length theatre play. I banged these out on an old, rickety, manual typewriter, writing and rewriting until I was fully satisfied with the finished product. Then, one by one, I posted off the manuscripts to selected entertainment executives and art directors. Off they went, one by one; and months later, back they came, one by one. They reminded me of great flapping birds coming home to roost, bringing with them polite rejection slips pinned to their title pages. Each time one returned, it made me cringe. These manuscripts would come through the letter-box, creating a despairing "plop" on the hall carpet. To this day, I can still hear the sound. By the end of 1988, it became increasingly evident that I was not destined to be a successful script writer. And so, I closed the book on that particular chapter.

Between 1989 and 1990, I took up work in the security business. By this time, I had decided to try novel writing, and reasoned that working nights would give me the opportunity to draft a novel in longhand. But this ambition, too, soon became obsolete. And, although I did not know it at the time, winds of change were beginning to blow through my life.

A Spontaneous Astral Journey

In July 1991, my wife and I were living and working in Florida. During our nine month stay there, I had one spontaneous out-of-body experience.

We were managing a mobile home park in St. Petersburg and living in the accommodation provided on site. We were also caretaking a mobile home in New Port Richie, about an hour's drive north of St. Petersburg, and would spend our weekends there. One Sunday night, after returning to St. Petersburg, I lay in bed wondering if I had switched off the immersion heater in the mobile home in New Port Richie. It worried me so much that I planned on driving back up the following evening to see if the heater was switched off.

Some time during the night, I discovered that I was standing in the mobile home in New Port Richie, by the fuse box where the heater switch was located. There was enough light in the room to see that the water heater switch was, indeed, in the "off" position. Once I had checked the switch, I "walked" into the living room; then I began to wonder what I was doing there. As if in response to my mental confusion, some other part of me said that my job there was finished, and that I should return to St. Petersburg. The following morning, I awoke with a clear recollection of the whole incident. I instinctively knew that I had had an out-of-body experience. I knew, also, that there was no further need to worry about the heater, or make an unnecessary journey to check it out.

Psychic Research

1992 (Dublin)

During my adult life, I had always had an interest in betting on horse and greyhound racing. Around 1985, I discovered that periods of "luck" coincided with periods of practising certain mind-training techniques. In the years that followed, I experimented a little with this, and saw that psychic power could, indeed, be used to foresee the winners of horse and greyhound races. For example, on one occasion, I used a particular method to make my selections before a trip to the greyhound track at Harold's Cross. From the selections I made before going to the races, I had the winner of the first race; the forecast (first and second) of the following six races; and the winner of the eighth race. When this psychic system worked, it really worked. But there was a snag: it never worked consistently on demand.

So, in 1992, I decided to research psychic power in order to understand how it worked (see also 'Experiments with Psychic Power'). In the course of this research, I spent long hours in deep meditation. During these periods, I often slipped into spontaneous states of altered consciousness, and, at these times, I was "contacted" by spirit beings who announced themselves as "guides." In the first half of the year, I met a number of different guides. For instance, there was one female, dressed in shimmering, pale blue robes, who introduced herself as "Thoth." Not that I suspect any connection, but I later discovered that there was also an Egyptian god of the same name – the god of wisdom and knowledge. I only met this particular guide twice. Her messages were of love, peace and harmony. Regretfully, around the end of the year, I accidentally formatted the computer's hard drive and wiped the record of her wisdom out of existence.

Around the autumn of 1992, I was approached by what I now call my "regular" Guides. Before this, I often doubted the validity of guides, in general, and, as a result, I did not embrace their wisdom whole-heartedly. I had frequently wondered if these entities were merely products of an overly fertile imagination. I theorised, too, that perhaps they were nothing more than fragments of my own personality that had split off and become autonomous in the psyche. But, after a number of meetings, I began to acknowledge my regular Guides as individual beings in their own right.

I asked their names, where they came from, and why they did what they were doing. (As I pointed out in the 'Introduction', I cannot divulge their names.) They told me that they were Tibetan Buddhist monks, who, through many earthly incarnations, had reached "enlightenment." And because of reaching enlightenment, they were given the choice of either reincarnating to teach on the physical plane of existence, or they could carry out their teaching from the astral dimension. They chose the latter.

What they told me was indeed plausible. From the time of our first meeting, I had wondered what nationality they were. Their facial features led me to assume they were from either Afghanistan or Mongolia. They presented themselves to me in the physical forms of their last incarnations: one was tall and lean with a furrowed, weathered face and close-cropped grey hair; the other was shorter and stockier, with a round, fresh-complexioned face and short hair, somewhat balding in front.

I asked why they had chosen to teach me, of all people. It was because of my luminosity, they said. When I questioned this statement, I learned that when spirit beings "look" at a person in the physical world, they, first and foremost, see the aura – the energy field that surrounds the person's body. Apparently, the luminosity of this energy field depends on the mindset of the individual. For example, a person with a rigid, materialistic outlook on life would be less luminous than a person with spiritual aspirations.

But I did not have any spiritual inclinations or knowledge of spirituality when I first encountered these Guides. When I pointed this out to them, they said that in my case it did not matter: it was my Spirit's destiny that created the right luminosity; therefore, I had the potential to become spiritual. I also had the potential to become a "channeller," and this was what interested the Guides most of all. From their point of view, to guide one person along the spiritual path was one thing, but for them to teach someone with the potential to channel their teachings and disseminate the information they had to impart was a bonus. When they explained this to me, I had no notion of what channelling was, nor did I deem it important enough to enquire at the time. However, two years later, I discovered, in the course of reading, that channelling was a way of bringing information from the non-material planes of existence by using psychic/spiritual channels. I learned, too, that this ability is not uncommon, but is something that is used regularly by many throughout the world. (When I speak of "Guides," from this point onwards, it is these two Tibetan Buddhist monks to whom I refer.)

Dreams of Death

In mid-November 1992, I had a vivid dream. In the dream, a funeral was taking place at the cottage where I had spent my younger days. There was a hearse parked by the roadside outside the cottage gate; I got a distinct feeling that the hearse and its driver were waiting for a coffin to be brought out from the cottage. A small, scattered group of people also stood by the roadside, waiting, apparently, for the hearse to load its cargo. Soon, a coffin emerged from the cottage door, carried by men unknown to me. When they were about to place the coffin inside the hearse, I asked the person next to me who had died. He said, 'Michael Connolly is dead.' On realising I was at my own funeral, I woke up.

The following night I had another vivid dream. Once again, I was at a funeral. This time the location had changed; I stood with a crowd of people around a freshly dug grave, watching a coffin being lowered into its depths. Again, the funeral took place in the graveyard of my home parish of yester-year. When the coffin had been lowered, and as the priest continued with the burial ceremony, I asked someone near me who was being buried. The reply was: 'Michael Connolly.' Once more, it seemed I had attended my own funeral.

Despite the unusual content and clarity of these dreams, they did not worry me. Analysing them from a psychological perspective, I came to the conclusion that each dream was a subconscious enactment of the death of some aspect of my character, or personality. Since I was satisfied with my state of health at the time, subconscious fears regarding my physical condition were not an obvious explanation.

However, about two weeks later, for days on end, I experienced a disquieting sense of foreboding. For the first time in my life I actually felt I was going to die. Night and day, the words "time" and "time running out" kept passing through my mind. What was most unsettling were the feelings of loss and sadness: I felt I had squandered the precious time I had spent on earth to date.

Finally, out of desperation and with some trepidation, I decided to venture onto the astral and seek counsel from the Guides.

Astral Counsel

End of November 1992

I went to the temple via an altered state of consciousness and, before long, one of the Guides arrived. I referred to feelings of death that I had been experiencing, and asked what was happening to me.

'We know what is happening to you. Your Spirit is preparing to withdraw,' he stated matter-of-factly.

'Does that mean I am going to die?' I asked, hoping that the word "withdraw" carried an alternative meaning.

'Preparing to withdraw,' he repeated. 'Whether or not it decides to do so depends on you. You are going the wrong way in life. The Spirit knows this. While incarnated in your body it sees its chances of fulfilling its destiny growing less and less (see 'Destiny' – Book II).

'What am I doing wrong? What am I supposed to do?' I whined.

'There are two things you must do. First, follow your aspiration towards spiritual development. It is your duty, and the duty of each individual on this planet, to evolve spiritually. You cannot hope to make spiritual progress if you live the way you are living. Your lifestyle is antithetical to spiritual progress. You must observe your actions and correct this fault.'

'How do I do that?' I enquired. 'By letting go. By letting go of all that is in your mind. Your mind, like the mind of every other human being, has been conditioned to think in a certain way – a way that is detrimental to wholesome progress. As a result of this conditioning, your ego-consciousness is overloaded with false notions about life and living. You think that the meaning of life is to be found in worldly ambition, wealth, prestige, success, and all the other illusions that are admired by the masses. If your consciousness remains fastened to these things, it will remain limited and deluded. It will never be free enough to see the reality of life.

'A mind that is fettered to false ideas and desires is like an uncleaned, glass dinner plate. The plate is covered with remnants of old food. If the dinner plate is not cleaned within a period of time, mould will begin to form on its contents. If it still remains uncleaned, the remnants of food will putrefy and the mould will spread. In the end, all that will remain is an unpleasant mess – a mess that will quickly contaminate any wholesome food that enters its proximity.

'Therefore, the plate needs to be cleaned. First, the old unwanted and useless remnants of food need to be scraped away, dislodged from the plate. After that, the plate needs to be washed thoroughly. When the plate is washed and dried what will you see on it?'

I had not been expecting the question, and had to think back for a moment on what the Guide had been saying. The image of a sparkling clean plate entered my mind's eye.

'Nothing,' I replied. 'When the plate is cleaned there is nothing on it.'

'Correct,' he said. 'And so it should be with any mind that intends to expand. First, its contents must be reduced to nothing; then, it has to be cleaned thoroughly. When the glass dinner plate reaches this state, the reality of life can be seen through it with crystal-clear clarity.

'And as I have already said, if the plate is left uncleaned, all it can ever hope to be is a jumbled collection of unpleasantness.'

'So, is there any particular method, or technique, involved in this letting go?' I asked. 'How do I reduce the contents of my mind to nothing?'

'First, you observe yourself. Observe your thoughts, emotions and actions. Observation will identify the creative thoughts, emotions and actions that spring from the Spirit. It will also show the thoughts, emotions, actions and reactions that arise out of habit. These are easy to pinpoint. They repeat themselves day after day, even though they are negative and damaging to the whole being. Habitual patterns of thinking, feeling and acting do not belong to your True Self. They have been imposed on you during the course of your life by external influences and, subsequently, you have learned to think, feel, act and react in a conditioned way. Therefore, you must rid yourself of old ways of thinking, feeling, acting and reacting. These patterns serve no other purpose than to keep you fettered to the same spot. And as long as you remain tied to the same spot [level of consciousness], there can be no advancement or expansion.'

'You mentioned creative thoughts, emotions and actions that arise from the Spirit. How are these identified?' I asked.

'Mainly by their spontaneity and purity. Any thought, desire, and ultimate action that stems from the Spirit is creative and expansive in a non-material way. That is, the desire of the Spirit is to expand the whole being, through learning by experience. Learning and acting are ways in which the Spirit expresses itself. The Spirit does not think in terms of material status or material gain. These concepts are nonsense to the Spirit.'

At this point I felt tired, and wanted to wrap up the discussion. 'What else should I do to fulfil the destiny of the Spirit?'

'You know what you are supposed to do, but you are not putting enough effort into it. Your destiny was made known to you years ago. Your main purpose in this incarnation is to write. If the spirit is not allowed to express itself in this way, then it will have to withdraw and incarnate again to achieve its aspirations.'

With that, the Guide turned his back and made his way towards the rear of the temple. I willed myself back to everyday consciousness, feeling somewhat relieved to be back in familiar surroundings. Though, now, not only was my mind uneasy with what the Guide had said, but I also remained as baffled as ever about what to write.

Within a short space of time, the Guide's words were forgotten. My concerns about dying had passed away, leaving a clear road to carry on living as I had always done.

A Tap from the Spirit

May 1993

In late April of 1993, I began to suffer severe chest pains. These pains became so bad that I could not even smoke a cigarette, and, for me, that was pretty bad. On the fourth of May, I collapsed and was brought to hospital where, before long, I ended up in the Intensive Care Unit. It transpired that I had viral pneumonia in both lungs.

During the sixteen-day stay in hospital, I brushed shoulders with death on two occasions. These two near-death experiences brought home to me the impermanence of life. Up until this time, I had treated my body as if it were indestructible; now I realised how easy it was to die. I realised, too, that when a person is close to drawing the final breath, the significance of wealth, status, and all the petty, mundane things we deem important quickly disappear into nothing, like a wisp of smoke. When I became well enough to sit up in bed and look at those around me in the hospital ward, I saw that I was not the only suffering individual in the world. In the bed across from mine was a man physically paralysed from a stroke; so paralysed that he could only move his eyes. In the opposite corner of the ward another man lay dying from cancer.

This man did die. And as his body was being wheeled out of the ward, I wondered how the man had lived his life. What great deeds had he done? What joys and sorrows had he experienced? Now it did not matter: that man's existence in this lifetime was over – end of story. Life went on. Lunch was served. And two hours later, another suffering person filled the emptiness of the dead man's bed. The whole scenario was like an ethereal dream.

Most poignant of all was the unique compassion of the nurses, doctors, hospital staff and even the patients themselves. It left me pondering why this compassion did not exist in the world outside. If someone here asked, 'How are you?' the question was not a vacuous salutation; the words came from the heart.

After leaving hospital and in the months that followed, recuperation came slowly. The infection had not quite cleared and, as a result, my energy level remained depressingly low. During this period, my strength was not sufficient to project the astral body. While in a restful reverie one day, however, I was "visited" by one of the Guides. He said that now was the time to devote myself seriously to the business of self-development, and that he and his counterpart would guide me through this process, if I so wished. He said that I had much to learn, and they had much to teach. However, the Guide pointed out, that the knowledge they wished to impart was not "new" knowledge; it had been around for thousands of years in one form or another. He told me that I must read books on psychology and, by doing so, I would begin to understand the nature of my own mind and the minds of others. He also said that I must observe, and focus on, myself; that I must become familiar with the contents of my mind, and how those contents determine my feelings and actions. Finally, the Guide recommended a way in which we could meet and communicate, without having to project the astral body to the temple.

The meeting place he suggested was what he referred to as "the boundary between the two worlds" – the physical and the astral. The Guide showed me a vision of this boundary, and told me that whenever I wished to make contact, all I had to do was visualise, and concentrate on, this meeting place. Little did I know that this boundary would play a pivotal role in the intriguing developments that lay ahead.

The Boundary between Two Worlds

The boundary between the two worlds is a band of energy consisting of three different layers. The first is like a thin wall of transparent silver-grey vapour; it is easy to see and pass through this particular energy layer. The third layer is also a like a thin wall and is semi-transparent and plum-coloured. When I say "semi-transparent," I mean that figures behind this wall would have to stand close to it in order to be seen from my standpoint; even then, their facial features would not be clearly defined. Lying between these two energy walls is a greenish-yellow strip of "land" about fifteen feet wide. At first glance, this greenish-yellow ground cover looks like a peculiar type of grass. But to the "touch" it does not feel like grass; it's texture is soft and malleable. My first impression was that, in terms of energy, this strip was a sort of no man's land: a frontier where one energy frequency finished and another began. It was on this strip, between the two energy walls, that many subsequent meetings with the Guides took place.

The Spirit Nuns

The month of July arrived and, as far as my health was concerned, it was very much a time of ups and downs: if I expended too much energy one day, I would have to stay in bed the next. Out of boredom, I decided to contact the Guides by focusing on the boundary between the two worlds. When I tried this, to my surprise, it was not the Guides who appeared. After a short period of visualising the boundary, the image of a nun become visible on the other side. With a wave of her arm, she motioned me to cross over. I was a little apprehensive about this at first. Up until now I had not passed beyond the plum-coloured wall and, as I understood it, the boundary was a meeting place only, not a place for exploration. The nun's gestures of invitation increased in urgency, so much so, that I forgot about my concerns and willed myself across. I felt myself passing through this plum-coloured energy wall; it felt like walking through a wall of water. On the other side, the nun greeted me by name and asked how I was feeling. Having found a willing ear, I began to relate the story of my recent bout of illness.

'Yes, we know,' she said, smiling benevolently. 'We have been praying for you.'

She introduced herself and gave a brief history of her background. She said that during her life on earth she had been a member of a particular Order of nuns in Ireland, and that she had passed over into the Spirit Realm in the early fifties. Because this person may have existed, I shall omit her real name, and refer to her as Sr. Theresa.

The first thing that struck me about Sr. Theresa was her character. It is rare, indeed, to meet someone with such an effervescent personality; she seemed to radiate an ineffable life-force. Of medium build, and about five-foot-six-inches tall, she had a round, friendly face. She wore glasses, and this surprised me. I had never seen anyone in the astral worlds wearing eye-glasses before. Sr. Theresa picked up what I was thinking.

'Oh, that's just a habit,' she laughed. 'Forgive the pun!' she added, tapping me on the arm. 'I carry on just as I did on earth. I always wore glasses, so I still wear them, even though I don't need them.'

'You said that you knew of my illness and that you were praying for me,' I urged.

'Yes, that's correct,' she answered. 'Not just me, but all of us.' She swept her arm towards a quadrangle of stone buildings a few hundred yards away. 'That's the convent over there,' she said. 'That's where we live, and pray, and carry out God's work.'

'What religious Order does the convent belong to?' I asked.

'No one in particular. The nuns that come and stay here are from different Orders. But, no matter. We are all the same here. We spend our days in prayer, as we always did. We offer up our prayers for the reversal of social ills, for people who are ill and for urgent causes.'

When Sr. Theresa had first mentioned that the nuns had been praying for me, I assumed that they were praying for me, personally; now I got the feeling that the nuns prayed for sick people collectively.

'We do both,' she said, in answer to my thoughts. 'First of all, we congregate every morning at the boundary between the two worlds. Then we pray to God to show us something to pray for. If we focus very hard, we are able to see into the earth dimension. We see places of danger and suffering; we also see into hospitals. That is how we saw you. Once we know what and who to pray for, then we carry on praying for that purpose throughout the day. It's hard work – but we love every minute of it,' she added with a charming smile.

When I heard about the nuns focusing on the boundary between the two worlds and being able to see into the earth dimension, I was reminded of the process of scrying, or crystal gazing. In this particular practice, by focusing on a speculum, such as a crystal ball, it is possible to see into the astral worlds. It seemed to me that what the nuns were doing was the same process in reverse.

'I'm glad that you are better,' she said. 'But we will continue to pray for you until you are completely well. Talking of prayer, why don't you join us in the chapel?'

Up until now, in keeping pace with the Sr. Theresa's conversation, I had not had the opportunity to examine my surroundings in detail. I looked at the boundary. From this side, the plum colour could be seen, but it was overlaid with a subdued sky-blue. This energy wall ran off in opposite directions across a vast, undulating, grassy plain. Where troughs occurred in the terrain, the wall curved slightly towards the earth dimension. Looking in all directions, I saw that the plain was devoid of trees or shrubs. I noticed, too, that an extraordinary glow emanated from the entire plain.

Sr. Theresa walked off towards the convent. When the thought of moving came to mind, I was at her side, "walking" along with her. Outside the convent buildings, we paused on the edge of a wide, circular slab of cut stones. Three stone steps led down into the circle. The stones looked like granite, but the nature of the stones was unimportant compared to their exquisite design. The joints of the stonework created the perception of concentric circles radiating out from a central point, and each ring of joints seemed to have an inherent "aliveness." When I shifted my vision, the perception of the circles faded into the background, giving way to a series of straight lines that also radiated out from the centre. The words "cosmic diagram" came to mind.

A straight path, constructed of the same stone, ran from the circle, widening as it went, to the convent's arched entrance. This led to a cobble-stone courtyard, in the centre of which a small tree grew in a wooden barrel.

Underneath the archway, to the right, was a heavy, maple door. This was one of the entrances to the chapel. As I walked through the door, I saw that it was supported by sturdy, black, iron hinges. We passed through a hallway; on the right stood a small, marble holy water font; opposite the font, on the left, was a tall statue of the Blessed Virgin with a candle burning at its feet. We entered the chapel. On the polished wooden floor, a strip of red carpet ran through the centre of the chapel all the way to the altar. On both sides of the building were three, arched, stained-glass windows. The chapel was almost full of nuns, kneeling in pews on either side, reciting the rosary.

We took our place in a pew at the rear. 'Stay for one decade of the rosary,' Sr. Theresa whispered. Before I knelt, I looked around me and saw that some nuns were dressed in black, some in white, and others in cream-coloured habits with black veils.

When prayers were over, Sr. Theresa accompanied me to the stone circle out front. 'Come and join us in prayer any time you want,' she said. 'We will continue to pray for you, but if you really want good health, you must change your lifestyle.'

I had no recollection of leaving the stone circle or making my way back through the energy wall. I simply returned to everyday consciousness, feeling elated by what had taken place.

During the summer of 1993, I visited the "astral convent" on five or six occasions. Each time, I was met and greeted by Sr. Theresa. We prayed together in the chapel, and, each time, she informed me of what or who that day's prayers were for. On my visits, I noticed that at some times the chapel was full of nuns, but other times only two or three were present.

Once, I asked if they had priests there, and if they ever had Mass in the chapel? Sr. Theresa replied that priests did sometimes say Mass there. But, she added, priests came and went. Some arrived, stayed briefly, and then went off to other "places." Other priests came but, after a period of time, decided to return to earth to carry out God's work.

On another occasion, Sr. Theresa mentioned Jesus. I asked if she had ever seen Jesus. Her response was: 'No, Jesus is higher up. He's with God in the God-Realm. We know He is there – we can feel His presence, so we don't have to see Him. We are happy to carry out His work here.'

Observing the Self

September 1993

The summer passed and autumn slowly set in. As the Guides had instructed, I had been reading psychology and found the subject fascinating. Throughout the summer, I had also devoted a good portion of time to the process of self-observation, and discovered, to my surprise, that this process had more merit than I assumed. Regular practice gradually revealed habitual patterns of negative thinking and feeling, of which I was unaware.

But information from the Guides remained scanty during this time. It was not for want of trying on my part. Many times, I tried consulting them about one thing or another, but they refused to answer my questions. Each time I queried something, all they had to say in reply was "focus on self." These words usually ended our meetings. In a way, this annoyed me. I did not fully comprehend their cryptic message "focus on self," so how was I to take action when I did not know what action to take? Finally, after much supplication, around the end of September, they explained.

'You are already doing what we advised you to do. You are focussing on yourself by observing yourself. So why do you want us to explain something you know how to do. Our advice in this matter is: do more of it. You have reached a stage in your development where you need to practice what we preach. In this case, you can only learn by doing. But it is your choice.'

The Power of Prayer

Following a visit to the astral convent, I asked the Guides about the efficacy of prayer.

'Prayer is powerful,' the Guide said. It invokes and directs spiritual power; not only in heaven, but also on earth. It achieves results. Prayer elevates consciousness to spiritual levels; that is, while the individual is engaged in the act of praying. But in order to do this [raise consciousness to spiritual levels], it is necessary to pray in a proper manner. Words alone are not sufficient.'

A moment passed as I waited for the Guide to continue. I then got the feeling that he was waiting for me to ask what he meant by "praying in the proper manner." Just as I thought of asking the question, he proceeded to answer.

'Perhaps I should first tell you how *not* to pray. That is, reciting words by rote. Anyone can recite words by rote and not pay attention to what they are saying. Many people do this. But this type of prayer is empty prayer. It has no power. For a prayer to have power, it is necessary to put your mind, heart and soul into the act of praying.

'The first step is to calm the system. Use rhythmic, deep breathing for a number of minutes until muscular tensions have left your body, and your mind and emotions have reached a calm state. When you are confident that your energy system has calmed, the next step is to develop a spiritual link with whichever Deity or Saint you are praying to. Picture this Spiritual Being clearly in your mind. Imagine that you are in the presence of this Being, and hold the image until you can feel a closeness – a closeness in proximity, or as a bond between you.

'Invoke the feeling of love: Universal Love. Remember that love is a powerful energy and the essence of God. This essence is both within and without. It can be felt in the heart chakra [located in the region of the physical heart]. Focus on the heart chakra until you can feel love. Imagine that your heart is open, and that Universal Love can flow in and out. But for the moment, it is flowing in; it is filling your heart.

'The next step is to exercise the key element in all prayer: *intent*. The exercises up until now have served to put you in touch with spiritual powers, internally and externally. You are now like an electrical appliance connected to the current, waiting for the switch to be thrown. And the switch, in this instance, is intent.

'Intent must be clear-cut and pure. By that, I mean that you must clearly visualise what you want your prayers to achieve. When intent is clear-cut and pure, and when your consciousness is connected to spiritual levels, spiritual power can travel along the line of intent, and will ultimately create the desired effect. In other words, your prayers will be answered.

'I must point out that there is a right way and a wrong way of intending. Say, for example, that you are praying for someone who is very ill. Your prayers are intended to ease the individual's suffering, but it is not wise to visualise that individual lying in bed suffering. When you send Universal Love and prayer, visualise the ailing individual leaving bed and walking off smiling, healthy and happy. That is the correct way to intend. Picture the situation exactly as you want it to be.'

'Can this method of praying be applied to all situations?' I asked.

'Yes,' answered the Guide. 'And it will produce positive results.'

I thought about destiny. I wondered if prolonged praying for someone could effect a change in, or alter the course of, the person's life.

'No,' he said. 'You cannot tamper with the destiny of another. Destiny is in the Spirit. But you can change an individual's attitude to life by prayer. Negative character traits, negative behaviour patterns and such are elements of the Ego. The Ego can be changed in any way that a person desires. The Ego, and all its contents [behavioural patterns, habits], can be eliminated entirely without threatening the survival of the individual.'

'Are you saying, then, that a naturally violent person can be changed into a non-violent person through the power of prayer?' I asked.

'Yes,' said the Guide. 'I will explain this to you again. When an individual prays, the act of praying puts the individual in touch with spiritual power. And when spiritual power is directed positively towards, let us say, a violent person, that positive spiritual power will enter, and act upon, the energy field of the violent person. But bear in mind the importance of intent. The individual who is praying must visualise the result that they want to effect. In other words, the individual, while in the act of praying, must, first of all, send love to the violent person; then, visualise that person behaving in a calm, happy and loving manner.

'There are two important points to remember. First, Universal Love is a force that has the capacity to nullify all negativity. Secondly, the power of prayer is not just confined to healing individuals; it is worthwhile, also, to pray for the healing of social ills, and the planet, Earth, in general.'

The year, 1993, came to an end. My six-month period of illness, during this particular year, had made me more receptive to spirituality and the concept of a spirit world. But towards the end of 1993, when my health was fully restored, I gradually "forgot" about the spiritual side of life, and temporarily ceased my journeys into the astral/spirit worlds.

The Human Energy System

In the spring of 1994, the Guides told me that in order to make any worthwhile progress I would have to study, and experiment with, my energy system – the chakras, in particular. At this point in time, although I knew what the aura and chakras were, this knowledge was limited. Over a period of months, I did as the Guides instructed.

Before I give an account of these results, it is necessary to have a basic understanding of the nature of the human energy system. Covering this subject in detail is beyond the scope of this book; indeed, many excellent books have been written on this subject alone (some of these are noted in the bibliography).

As we are all well aware, each of us on this earth has a material body. This body is evident to the physical senses: it can be seen, heard, touched, tasted and smelled. Indeed, the majority of us identify "self" with the physical body, and continuously refer to it as "I." For example, most people use the phrase, "when I die," when they really mean, "when my physical body dies." This ego-based perception has become so entrenched in Western culture that when the subject of subtle, energy bodies crops up, it is often greeted with disbelief and, sometimes, derision.

The reason for this attitude is quite understandable. After all, the subtle, energy field – the aura – is not palpable under normal circumstances. It can, however, be seen by individuals who have developed clairvoyant or psychic sight, and it can be sensed by healers. For thousands of years, mystics and seers have used clairvoyant/psychic vision to view the aura; it can also be photographed using a technique called "Kirlian photography."

The aura is an envelope of energy that works through, and surrounds, the physical body. It is made up of energy layers, with each layer vibrating at a frequency higher than the one "below" it. It can extend anywhere from six to thirty-six inches beyond the surface of the physical body, depending on the mental/emotional state, physical health and energy level of the human being. The aura is made up of a variety of colours, each colour representing a particular frequency of energy. The colour configuration of the aura is not consistent, by any means: it can change from one minute to the next, depending on the thoughts and feelings of the individual.

Before we discuss the colours of the aura and chakras, let us take a look at the energy layers, or "bodies," that comprise the totality of the aura. Beginning with the most refined, these are: the causal (Soul/Spirit) body, the astral body, the mental body, the emotional body, and the etheric body.

The causal (Soul/Spirit) body is the principal link between ego-consciousness and God-consciousness. It is the core, the nucleus, of our being. According to my Guides, the Soul is the subconscious mind; the Spirit is the unconscious mind. These two interactive aspects of psychic/spiritual energy are what is traditionally called the "causal" body. It is the "vehicle" by which each of us can experience the Divine, if we so choose. The vibrational frequency of the causal body is the highest on the energy vibration scale.

The astral energy spectrum encompasses the mental and emotional frequencies of energy. This energy field is denser than the psychic/spiritual, and responds not only to impressions from the psychic/spiritual level, but also to perceptions from the physical senses. Inspiration, psychic impulses, logical thoughts, memory, intuition and emotional feelings – all become conscious in the astral energy field. In this way, when the astral body is projected, consciousness travels with it.

The densest non-material energy "body" of all is the etheric. Just as the causal body interacts with, and interpenetrates, the astral body, the astral body interacts with, and interpenetrates, the etheric. The etheric body can extend from one to three inches from the surface of the skin, and is latticed with lines of energy known to practitioners of Traditional Chinese Medicine as "meridians." The etheric body is also dotted with nodal points and energy vortices of varying size and intensity. These are called the "chakras."

The chakras are small whirlpools of energy located in the etheric electromagnetic fields that surround the human body. In the human system there are seven primary chakras, and it is these chakras, in particular, that we rely on for our mental, emotional and physical well-being. The following table lists each chakra and its colour and position relative to the human body. Not all authors fully agree on the colours traditionally assigned to each chakra. This is possibly because colours, or energies, when seen with psychic/clairvoyant vision, are not always positioned where they should be. For example, the red energy, associated with the Base chakra can, in some individuals, be displaced, and can be seen in the upper chakras, up to and including the Throat chakra. The energies (colours) of the human aura are continually affected by our thoughts and emotions, and are, therefore, in a constant state of flux.

Chakra	Colour	Position
1. Root or Base	Red	Base of the spine
2. Sacral	Orange	3 Finger-widths below the navel
3. Solar Plexus	Yellow	3" Above the navel
4. Heart	Green	Heart area
5. Throat	Blue	Adam's apple
6. Third Eye	Violet	Between the eyebrows
7. Crown	White	Top of the head

Experimenting with the Chakras

Once I had familiarised myself with the nature of the chakras, the Guide suggested that, in a meditative state, I should focus on and learn to sense each chakra; in other words, develop a perceptual awareness of these energy centres. One of the Guide's exercises involved sensing a chakra, then willing it to move from side to side, so that its movement could be perceived. This perception, I discovered, was not so much one of movement, but of a resistance by the chakra when it was pushed towards one side or the other. The Guide issued a strict warning not to go overboard with this particular exercise because the chakras were easily displaced. Displacement of chakra energy can result in mental, emotional and physical disease.

After a number of practice sessions, I began to "feel" the energy centres without difficulty. At various times of the day and night, I would often experience a vibrating, or tingling, outside the body in the region of one chakra or another. Once, I experienced a peculiar pain about three inches outside my body in the Solar Plexus centre. This pain lasted a number of hours and was extremely uncomfortable.

I asked the Guide what was happening to me. He said that the chakra system was beginning to open, and, because the system had been damaged by rigid thinking and negative experiences over the years, it would take some time to clear the warps and blockages so that energy could flow freely. He suggested that when preparing to meditate I should position my body so that all the chakras lined up. This entailed lying flat, feet together, and imagining a straight, thin line of energy running from the top of my head to my inner ankle bones. With this line in mind, I had to manoeuvre my body until the entire system felt like a straight line. And, at that point, in order to create a balance, I was to focus on all seven chakras at once, giving the same amount of attention to all. This exercise did, indeed, produce a feeling of being totally "in tune."

However, throughout the summer of 1994, while practising these exercises, not all my experiences were pleasant. At times, during the practices or shortly afterwards, I experienced intense and uncharacteristic emotions, like anger and melancholy, for instance.

Again I consulted the Guide.

'What you are experiencing is a release of blocked energies. That is what these emotions are – energies. And that is what all emotional feelings are: they are energies. The only power emotional feelings can have is the power you give them. When an emotion arises within you, simply observe it, recognise it for what it is, and let it go.'

As autumn approached, I had another unusual experience. For days, I had a strange sensation throughout my entire body. It would be more accurate to say that this sensation was not just within my body, but also outside the skin's surface.

When I asked the Guide about this phenomenon, I was told that the unusual feeling was due to the exercises I had been practising. He said that the vibration rates of the etheric and astral bodies were being refined. He went on to say that once my physical body became accustomed to being surrounded by these finer vibrations, I would no longer feel them. Unless, of course, I refined them yet again.

Another point that may be of interest to researchers in this field, is one that relates to the age-old debate about the exact location of what we call "mind." In scientific and medical circles, there is a convincing amount of evidence to indicate that the mind is located in the brain. However, among mystics, clairvoyants (especially aura readers), spiritual healers and chakra energy healers there is an equal amount of evidence that says it is not. Those who deal exclusively with the human energy system suggest that "mind," as we know it, – intellect, memory, etc. – is contained within, and distributed throughout, the auric energy field.

While practising "sensing" the chakras one day, I focussed, in particular, on the Solar Plexus chakra. At the same time, I suddenly, and inadvertently, slipped into an altered state and found myself back in my childhood. This was not simply a case of remembering, or observing, a recollection of the following incident; I actually existed in the memory.

There was a particular tree I used to climb, which grew beside an out-house. Now, I was back in the tree, sitting on one of its branches. I saw the bark and withering leaves of the tree; I felt the breeze blowing through my hair; I saw the moss growing on shed's roof. In a nutshell, every detail was as clear as if I were living it – in the moment. I felt bored, and spotting the white, plastic football lying on the grass by the end of the cottage, I climbed down from the tree, went over and picked up the ball. I noticed an area on the plastic ball where my aunt had "welded" a puncture with a hot fire-poker. I began to play with the ball, bouncing it up and down...

I returned to ordinary consciousness, overwhelmed by this experience. Even my travels to other dimensions of existence failed to evoke the amazing feeling associated with this episode. No words could describe this feeling; the nearest I can come is to say that I had a profound perception of timelessness. There was no difference in time, space, or awareness, between me in the memory, and me, the adult, almost forty years later. On analysing the contents of this episode, I realised that the memory of that white football, and especially the plastic "weld," had never before surfaced in my adult recall. It had been completely forgotten.

What had triggered this memory? What had caused, not just a recollection, but an actual reliving of it? At first I dismissed the episode as a psychic idiosyncrasy. But, some weeks later, while practising the same exercises on the

Solar Plexus chakra, it happened again.

This time, in the "memory" I was older, about eleven years of age. I sat at the kitchen table doing my homework. We had a budgerigar, at the time, who liked to roam freely around the house. Most of all, she liked walking around on the kitchen table, especially when I was engaged in scribbling compositions. I always tried to finish my homework as quickly as possible so that I could escape the temporary tedium, and take myself off to the freedom of the fields. As I scribbled, the budgie, through one beady eye, would watch the quick erratic movements of the pen-handle; whenever I slowed down, she would fly at the pen-handle, grabbing it in her beak. A "tug-of-war" would ensue between the budgie and myself, both trying to gain control of the pen.

Once again, I participated in this long-forgotten memory. And, while in the memory, from time to time I would look up from writing and see every detail of the kitchen and the garden outside the kitchen window. It was as if I were actually there.

On returning to ordinary consciousness, I once more experienced a perception of timelessness. Not only that, but there was also an indescribable euphoria: it was as if I were privy to a magical state, an eternal joy and a wonder of youth. However, these perceptions did not last long. By the time the conscious mind and sensory faculties were fully operational, they had disappeared.

Both these "flashbacks," however, did have a down side. In both cases, for a couple of days afterwards, I felt "incomplete": mildly dissociated from my perception of everyday reality. For this reason, I discontinued this particular avenue of experimentation.

Before we move on, I would like to reiterate the Guide's warning. Do not, under any circumstance, undertake experiments of this nature without the company of an experienced group or competent teacher.

Earthbound Spirits

I lay on the bed and, after about forty-five minutes of rhythmic breathing and concentration, reached the borderline of an altered state of consciousness. Then, I carried out the exercise of mentally getting up off the bed and walking around the room. I visualised myself complete with a body – a replica of my own physical body – and then proceeded to walk slowly around the room, noting all the items it contained, especially the details of each item.

Before long, I was conscious of myself walking down the hallway and out the front door. (This was not a part of the practice schedule; my consciousness had now projected.) My next recollection was of walking along a familiar street about half-a-mile away from where I lived. I wondered what I was doing on this street: was I going to the store for something, or was I coming home from the store? While trying to figure this out, and while trying to mentally establish which direction I should be travelling in, a tramp appeared out of nowhere and ran up to me (see 'Life after Death' – Book II). He was a jolly fellow, full of effusive chat, but his ragged appearance caused me some embarrassment. I did not want to be seen talking to this fellow; as a matter of fact, I felt a lot of embarrassment. This feeling seemed more acute in the out-of-body state than it normally would in the physical body. The tramp was now so overjoyed by our meeting that he tried to embrace me. This extravagant display of affection increased my feeling of embarrassment to the point of panic. In the process of willing myself away from him, I inadvertently returned to my physical body.

Later that night, I decided to have another go at projecting. In a way, I wanted to carry on where I had left off earlier, but without the company of the wayward tramp. My goal was to familiarise the conscious mind with the out-of-body state so that it would become accustomed to, and rationally function in, that condition.

I carried out the preliminary exercises and visualised the stretch of street I wanted to be at. It happened. Suddenly, I was there, in the exact spot where I had met the tramp. The tramp was absent from the scene this time, but I saw two aggressive looking characters coming towards me on the opposite side of the street. In normal, everyday consciousness I tend to avoid such people, and this built-in aversion urged me return home to my physical body. Unfortunately, I had been spotted by the two undesirables, and sensed that going back towards home would serve to show my fear. Quickly, the pair crossed the street and confronted me, demanding money for pizza. When I told them I did not have any money, they attacked me, as I had suspected they would. The shock of being attacked brought me straight back to my physical body with a tremendous jolt.

The Astral Cardinal

16 May 1995

I went to visit the nuns in the astral convent and, as usual, I was welcomed by Sr. Theresa. She asked why I had stayed away for so long, and the way she said it caused me to feel guilty for my long absence. As before, we prayed in the chapel, and, afterwards, as we stood in the stone circle outside, I asked why the convent was so isolated. She told me that all the nuns there liked privacy, just as they had liked privacy on earth; that bustling cities were antithetical to proper prayer and contemplation. I asked if there was a city nearby. She answered that there was one about three hundred miles away, and that this city played host to a replica of the Vatican, and, she added, '. . . they might even have a Pope there now.'

Expressing a desire to visit this city, I immediately found myself flying through the air at great speed. I do not recall entering a building, but I ended up in a large, ornate room in which a stately, white-haired man in cardinal's regalia stood.

'Sit down,' he said, pointing to a carved, high-backed chair, which was covered in red velvet and edged with gold fringe.

'Where am I?' I asked.

'You are in an astral dimension,' he replied. 'A lot of souls come to this dimension. They come when they leave the earth plane.'

I wondered if this place were some kind of heaven. The man understood what I was thinking.

'You are wondering if this is Paradise. It is not. If you want to find Paradise you will have to ascend to the higher worlds. This dimension is a sort of stop-over, a resting place.

I began to receive mental impressions of what the dimension was like: I saw an image of a busy city outside. Again, he knew what was in my mind.

'Yes,' he said, 'it's an exact replica of earth. Every single thing that exists on earth exists in this world also...' He turned and smiled, and, making a sweeping gesture with his left arm, added, '. . . even the Vatican.'

'Is there a Pope here,' I asked, thinking that perhaps the souls of past Popes came to reside here.

'No. When I arrived, this place [the Vatican building] was empty; devoid of a Papal presence, I mean.'

'And who are you?' I enquired.

'I am a Vatican Cardinal. At least I was during my past life on earth. I am going back to earth again as soon as a suitable incarnation arises.'

I was on the verge of asking him what he meant by a "suitable incarnation," but he anticipated my question.

'Incarnation is a tricky business. I am waiting for an incarnation that will provide me with an ecclesiastical life. I have a job to do on earth – a mission. So, I am waiting.'

I wondered why there was no Pope in the Vatican.

'From what I hear,' the Cardinal said, 'Popes do not stay here for long. They rest here before moving on to higher worlds.'

'What are those worlds like?'

'I do not know,' he answered. 'I have never travelled any further than here. There's no use going to higher dimensions if you intend reincarnating. This is the closest dimension to earth. I can keep an eye on things from here.'

'But is it possible for the souls of ordinary people to go to higher dimensions, or are those dimensions reserved for spiritual people only?' I asked.

'I do not know for certain,' he answered. 'I would guess that the higher worlds are for spiritually evolved people, but I cannot say for sure because I have not seen these dimensions. But "ordinary people," as you put it, come and go from here all the time. They emigrate – they emigrate and move on. That is what we say in this world when people are not here anymore.'

I asked him if there were other countries in this world, like on earth.

'Again, I do not know,' he said. 'I suppose there must be. Sometimes people who emigrate come back; sometimes soon after they leave, sometimes a long time after.'

'But don't these people say where they've been?' I asked.

'I'm not sure they know where they have been. It's like they get amnesia about where they moved to. They just come back and carry on where they left off. Nobody takes any notice.'

At that point I was drawn back to waking consciousness.

Other Out-Of-Body Experiences

After lying on the bed practising the preliminary exercises for astral projection, I slipped into an altered state of consciousness. The next thing I knew, I was standing in the bathroom, looking at myself in the mirror. The image I saw in the mirror was exactly like me, except for the fact that I looked as if I had been carved from a block of silver-white marble. The mirror-image was not wearing clothes, and this highlighted its unusual appearance. Under normal circumstances, this sight would have been startling, but for some reason, my linear/logical mind did not find it peculiar.

The "me" in the mirror suddenly materialised and stood in front of the "me" who was looking into the mirror. For a fraction of a second, he looked directly into my eyes; his gaze was relaxed, yet penetrating. It was as if he were trying to understand who I was. He then brushed past me and walked off down the hallway, throwing some comment over his shoulder. At this point, I looked at the "me" standing in the bathroom. This "body" was transparent and colourless; the outline of my limbs were barely discernible. At that instant, I experienced a split in consciousness: I was simultaneously standing in the bathroom and walking down the hallway; I could actually see both locations at the same time. Something within informed me to catch up with the "me" in the hallway; intuitively, I felt that letting this "body" get away from my consciousness in the bathroom would have disastrous results. I do not remember leaving the bathroom, but my next experience was of being "reunited" with the "me" outside the front door.

Yet again, my consciousness split. I became aware of being outside the front door and lying in bed. The latter awareness gradually assumed supremacy, and I returned to ordinary consciousness. (N.B. From an analytical viewpoint, all I can deduce from this episode is that the silver-white "me" that materialised in front of the bathroom mirror was my etheric body, and the "me" consciousness observing the etheric body was my astral body. Hence, the perception of urgency from within – the Soul/Spirit perhaps – to reunite both energy vehicles.)

I was still in a deeply relaxed state, which is perfect for projection, so I decided to try again. Within a short time, I was out-of-body, walking down the hallway once again. This time, I turned into the living room – something I had not intended to do. I went to the front window and looked out, still wondering why I was there. My consciousness was sluggish; it felt like my mind wanted to go asleep. The struggle with trying to "remember" what was happening brought me back to my physical body, and, as I became fully con-

54

scious, I felt an undulating sensation all along the surface of my skin. This particular sensation was entirely new to me at the time. It felt like something within my physical body was loosening.

25 May 1995

Out-of-body, I walked along a busy Dublin street during morning rush hour, heading towards the city centre. Everything I looked at – the cars, buses, buildings and people – was sharply defined; it was as if they all reflected sunlight. I was so absorbed in observing all around me that my consciousness did not question why I was there or where I was going. I turned right, onto another main street and, as I turned the corner, a couple of youths on bicycles were speeding along the footpath. One of the bikes, as it passed, swiped the side of my left thigh, almost knocking me down. I snapped back to waking consciousness immediately. On my thigh, I could still "feel" the sensation where the bike had brushed against me.

27 May 1995

I lay on the bed reading. Drowsiness descended and since this condition is conducive to entering an altered state of consciousness, I grabbed the opportunity. In a short time, I sensed a cincture of energy around my head. It felt like a wreath made of dried leaves; I could even "feel" the leaves rustling about an inch from my scalp. Instantly, I found myself looking down on a mountain range from a height of about twenty-thousand feet. I saw the mountain range in great detail and noticed how it jutted out into the sea to form a peninsula. The vision changed abruptly and I was now standing on a street close to home. A middle-aged woman walked towards me on the same side of the street. She was about five-foot-ten-inches tall, of stocky build, and had bobbed, dark-brown hair. She wore a knee-length, light-grey raincoat and flat shoes. I had never seen this woman before, yet something told me that she had the result of the Lotto draw – which, by the way, had not yet taken place. With a mischievous grin she said, 'If you had done the Lotto, you would've had four numbers up.' At this point, I returned to waking consciousness.

Before we move on, I would like to draw attention to the fact that this was the first time I had managed to project my consciousness forward in time. This particular projection happened in the early afternoon; yet, during the projection, when I met the brown-haired woman, I had a distinct feeling that the time was around 8:45 p.m. The Lotto draw takes place around 8 p.m. On meeting the woman, I felt that she had watched the Lotto draw on television, and that she knew the result. When I awoke from the projection, it crossed my mind that I should get up, go to the local store, and play the Lotto. I began to think about what numbers to play, and I got a feeling that the sequence of numbers I had played in the prior Wednesday night's draw contained the four winning numbers mentioned by the woman in the projection. As I pondered this point, I drifted back into an altered state.

My consciousness returned to the exact same spot where I had stood in the previous projection, but, this time, the dark-haired woman had crossed the street and was walking away from me. Sensing that she was about to disappear into an apartment block nearby, I shouted at her to tell me which four numbers of mine had come up in the Lotto draw. As she faded from my focus of attention, she called out, 'The four fours.'

Snapping back to waking consciousness, I saw that the time was 3:20 p.m. I did not understand what the woman had meant by "the four fours," nor did I give the matter any further thought. Perhaps it is merely coincidence, but the numbers drawn in the Lotto that evening did contain four fours. The numbers were: 4, 14, 18, 35, 36, 40, and the bonus number, 41.

30 May 1995

This morning, I awoke around daylight (4:30 a.m.) and decided to practice. Before long, I projected and found myself in a forest clearing, sitting at a low, rectangular altar stone. It was situated about eight inches off the ground; its perimeter was surrounded by small, leafy plants. I felt in harmony with the situation and something within me suggested that I should chant. This chant was supposed to be some kind of key that opened a doorway to yet another dimension. I started to sing. The sound was a mixture of American Indian chanting and sonorous, Gregorian chant. I had never before heard a sound like it; to my ears it seemed magical. The sound came not only from my mouth, but also emanated from my entire being. I seemed to know the words and melody, and, as I chanted, the sound increased in both intensity and harmony. It engulfed me so completely that I could not differentiate between myself and the sound. Simultaneously, I was both "me," the conscious entity, and "me," the sound. The feeling was one of absolute harmony, a condition I had never experienced in everyday reality.

7 June 1995

Today, I asked my regular Guides why I met the nuns and the Cardinal on the astral planes; I asked if it was because of my Roman Catholic upbringing. The Guide dismissed my suggestion, saying that I could meet with individuals from any religion I pleased. He said that in the Spirit worlds there was no difference between religions: all religions were one and the same; they all had a common goal, and that goal was to serve God.

My next recollection was of travelling through a jungle, where I met a man dressed in a bright-red robe. He looked like a Buddhist monk and indicated that I should follow him. Soon, we came to a clearing in the centre of which was a large, circular slab of cut stone. Leading into the circle was a set of stone steps at each quadrant. I saw that this stone construction was situated in front of a cave and, although I could not see inside, I got the impression that the cave was some kind of temple. I noticed, too, that the design of the stone-work was the same as that of the stone circle outside the "spirit nuns" convent. The monk now stood at the mouth of the cave, and with repeated waves of his left arm, he invited me to go in. On entering, I saw a gold statue of an Oriental god at the far end of the cave. It was surrounded by lit candles, and sitting in front of the candles was a group of monks. The monks had their backs turned towards me, but, despite not seeing their facial expressions, I felt a warming welcome emanating from each of them. One monk turned and threw me a cushion; it had a red silk cover, with a gold tassel at each of the four corners. As I caught the cushion in mid-air, I experienced a jolt, like an electric shock.

I understood that the cushion was an invitation to sit and meditate. I sat, wondering what I should meditate on. The monk who had ushered me into the cave suggested that I meditate on one of the four elements. On the wall of the cave, in my line of vision, was the image of a silvery-white crescent moon turned on its back, and, from books I had read on the Tattva symbols, I knew that this was the symbol of water. This "knowing" did not occur on an intellectual level, but came from somewhere deep within me.

After a second or two of looking at the crescent-shaped symbol, I became conscious of myself in the element of water. I was submerged, travelling along a river bed or an ocean floor, surrounded by fish and sea creatures of all kinds. This perception changed and, once again, I was in the cave. But now I was not sitting: I lay stretched out on my back. One of the monks had a copper disc, about nine inches in diameter, which he placed over my solar plexus area. He told me to focus on the feeling of power coming from that chakra. I immediately experienced a vortex of energy between my body and the disc. This energy lifted the disc, causing it to float about four inches above my stomach. I was intrigued by this phenomenon; I never imagined I had so much power. The monk told me to work on, and develop, this potential power, which, he said, could be used for both levitation and the transportation of the physical body over great distances.

I returned to ordinary consciousness and evaluated the content of my experience. I thought about what my own Guide had said about all religions being one and the same. I must have drifted off to sleep at that point and, as I awoke shortly afterwards, a male voice inside my head clearly said: 'The only division between human beings is a lack of understanding.'

9 June 1995

On this journey, I walked along the street of a foreign town. "Foreign" was a perception evoked by the style and architecture of the buildings. It had the "feel" of a small town in southern California or northern Mexico, yet all the inhabitants had a characteristic Nordic appearance. Groups of people stood around talking on street corners, and, as I walked along, I drew unfriendly glares. The way they stared made me wonder what was wrong with me: I felt like a person with two heads. By the time I had reached the busier centre of the town, I became convinced that everyone in the place was a little crazy. This was not attributed particularly to the actions of the people; it was more an intuitive feeling. I felt increasingly uncomfortable, on edge, and regretted not having turned around and bolted out of there when I first realised that something was amiss with the general population. It was now too late to go back to the outskirts of the town, as doing so would mean having to face the hostile glares all over again. It came to mind that perhaps I might be able to hire a taxi in the town centre, and that the taxi would take me safely beyond the town's limits.

I crossed the street to a small shopping mall built of yellow bricks. Rationality had told me that taxis queued for customers outside such shopping centres, but there were no taxis parked outside this one. The thought of phoning a cab brought me into a brick-built arcade to look for a telephone. There was a crowd in the arcade and most of these people behaved unpredictably. It was as if they were stoned on alcohol or drugs of some kind, yet, their eccentric carry on smacked more of chronic insanity, than of temporary intoxication.

A gang of young men hung around a paint-flaked, wooden bench, eyeballing me resentfully. As I approached, I could see that they were talking about me and planning something. My initial apprehension now turned to unadulterated fear. One of the young men disengaged himself from the group and belligerently swaggered over to me. He asked for money. I extracted all the spare change I had in my pocket, and saw that I had just enough to phone for a taxi. The youth became verbally abusive. In an attempt to defuse this potentially dangerous situation, I apologised profusely for not having money to give him. He said, 'We know your type of people – you're all the same.' With that, he walked off.

I turned quickly and went in the opposite direction. By now, I was almost in a state of panic. I had no idea how to get home, but that was the least of my worries. My immediate intention was to get away from the crazies. The intensity of this intention caused my consciousness to project yet again.

The next thing I knew, I was out of the town and in the heart of a countryside surrounded by rolling hills and grassy valleys. I walked along a narrow road flanked by stone walls. There were no trees, so I could see that the road snaked across the hills and valleys. I felt that "home" lay beyond a distant mist-capped mountain range. From where I was positioned on the side of a small hill, and because of the road's meandering, I saw that cutting across three or four fields was the shortest walking route to the next hill. On my journey across one of the fields, a black and white cow broke through some fencing and came running for me. As I sprinted towards a ditch, some hundred yards away, I could hear the cow's hoofs thundering along behind me. I do not remember climbing the ditch; one minute I was at field level, the next, I was safely on top of the ditch. The cow stood below me, winded and snorting heavily.

I looked up and saw two men in the adjacent field, running towards me. At first, I thought their intention was to chase me off their land, but it transpired they had run to rescue me from the cow. They introduced themselves, not by name, but as father and son, owners of the land I stood on. The father was a wiry, gaunt man with a deeply lined, weather-beaten face. I did not pay much attention to the clothes he wore, except for the brown, felt hat. The son was a burly fellow, at least a head taller than his father. He wore a checked, peaked cap, and I noticed that he wore leather, laced boots. What intrigued me most about the son was his eyes: they were dark, cold and emotionless.

The father did the talking, and, as he talked, I noticed that both of them scrutinised me strangely, as if I were some kind of peculiar creature. This surreptitious, yet thorough, visual examination reminded me of the stares I had received in the crazy town. The father apologised for the cow's behaviour and insisted that I be his guest. He told me that he wanted to atone for the actions of his mad cow, and all he could offer me was hospitality. As he went through this seemingly sincere spiel, conspiratorial looks shot back and forth between father and son.

As we walked across the fields to the farmhouse, I realised that the cow was not the only mad living being on the farm. The farmer's son now acted strangely. As he walked, he skipped and danced about, waving his arms in air and gesticulating wildly to no one in particular. It was as if he were using semaphore to send silent messages to some invisible being on the distant mountain-top. The father paid little, if any, attention to the shenanigans of his son; apparently he saw nothing unusual in this bizarre behaviour.

The farmhouse and surrounding farmyard lay in a small valley. There were no walls or fences around it. The house itself was white-walled, two-storeyed and thatched. There was an odd-looking tractor parked in the yard.

In the farmhouse yard, the father, walking ahead of me, emulated his son's odd behaviour. It flashed into my mind that he wanted to turn around to see if I were hesitant about entering the house, and I momentarily sensed that he did not want to make his observation obvious. Suddenly, he paused in mid-stride, gave a 360° twirl in the air, looked directly at me, then carried on walking towards the house as if nothing had happened.

Inside the house, the farmer showed me to the ground floor guest-room. The son had gone back outside; by now, I felt extremely ill at ease. Everything that had taken place since meeting the farmer and his son had been too staged.

I could not guess at what they were up to, but I got a psychic impression that I might be held in the farmhouse against my will.

The guest room was simply furnished. I sat on the bed and, as soon as the farmer left the room, began contriving a plan to escape through the window. My intention now was to put distance between myself and my "hosts." As I stood to examine my intended escape route, a girl, carrying a pad and pen, entered the room. She seemed to be in awe of me. She was about medium height, of stocky build and with medium-length, straight, blond hair. She introduced herself as "the farmer's daughter" and asked what I would like for dinner. Before I could answer, she proffered the pad and pen, and asked for my autograph, saying that they didn't get many of my kind visiting the locality. From her speech and actions, I could see that she was almost as eccentric as her sibling. Sensing it would be unwise to use my own name, I scribbled a fictitious name on the pad, then enquired what she meant by "my kind." To that, she answered, 'Alien.' She said that she knew I did not like being there, and she felt sorry for me. Not for the position I was in now, but for the experiments her father and brother might carry out in the future, using me as a guinea pig.

From the look of consternation on her face, I did not dare imagine what those "experiments" might be. I took advantage of her sympathy and asked if she would help me escape. She agreed, provided I promised to come back and visit her from time to time. Needless to say, I made the promise, but with no intention of keeping it. The girl left the room, and, shortly afterwards, her face appeared at the guest-room window. She opened the window from the outside; it swung outwards. The last thing I remember was squeezing myself out through the window. The sheer willpower involved in the intention to escape brought my consciousness safely back to my physical body.

11 June 1995

I had read one time that it was possible to project one's consciousness to other planets in the universe. When I first came across this piece of information, the idea struck me as ludicrous. But now, my thinking was not so limited. I decided to give this a try.

Using visualisation, I pictured myself leaving the planet, Earth, and travelling further and further into the galaxy. My next awareness was of standing on a flat, barren landscape. It looked as if it were composed of greyish rock, but with an inherent luminescence. Above, the star-filled sky was an ineffable, royal blue. The scene reminded me a summer's dawn in our own world.

Suddenly, a small flying object appeared from nowhere and hovered about thirty yards away. As I watched, the object dispatched a circle of seven small spheres of light, like miniature stars. These "stars" proceeded to orbit the hovering object in a clockwise direction, steadily increasing their speed. It seemed that this whirling speed created a centrifugal force around the central object. A ball a visible energy materialised within the ring of "stars" and increased in density, enveloping the central object. This energy propelled the circle of stars towards me. At first the circle widened, fanning out as if some force had exploded in the centre of the circle. Then the circle rapidly diminished, and all seven stars coalesced into one small ball of brilliant white light. As the ball of light came towards me, I turned to run, but tripped and fell. Before I could get up off the ground, I felt the light entering the back of my head. There, it began to harmonise with knowledge already in my consciousness. I got a distinct feeling that the light had an intelligence of its own, and that its purpose in entering my head was to learn the contents of my consciousness. The episode did not last long, and, all in all, it was not an unpleasant experience.

January 1997

We have a cat who sleeps all day and roams around at night. When he wants to be let in, he comes to the bedroom window and makes his presence known. This particular night, it was on my mind that the cat would come to the window to be let in. In my sleep, I thought I heard a noise and got up to see if it was the cat. I opened the window and leaned all the way out, trying to see where the cat was. No cat. I spent a moment or two looking at the beautiful night outside. The stars were twinkling in the heavens; the moon had bathed the back garden in silver. I drew back in and, when I went to latch the window, I saw that it was already latched. Returning to bed, I wondered how I had closed the window and not remembered doing it. Shortly afterwards, the cat did come to the window, and I got up (physically) to let him in. The scene outside was the same as I had seen earlier. Now, I realised why I had no recollection of closing the window after I had first looked out. Apparently, in my astral body, I had leaned all the way out through the closed window, and observed the scene outside.

25 May 1997

While in an altered state, I felt my consciousness being pulled. Then, there was a sense of movement. First, I encountered coloured geometrical shapes: squares, circles, triangles, ellipses. It was difficult to determine whether I was travelling through the coloured shapes, or if the shapes were travelling through me. These shapes gave way to a vast plane of magnificent colours. I had never before seen such vivid and vibrant colours. They were in constant movement. I watched streaks of yellow and pink flash across a background of red and green; blobs of blue, like bubbles, erupted from the red and green, then quickly receded. Finally, the blues, yellows and pinks disappeared, and I was left viewing the movement, the interplay, between red and green. Red was on the left; green on the right. They pushed against each other like two stormy seas. Sometimes the green pushed the red to the left, almost eliminating it from the scene. Then the red would push its way back and assume superiority. For what seemed like a long time, I watched the sea of red and the sea of green battling for supremacy. When I realised a battle going on before my eyes, I got the feeling that the lesson was at an end. At that point, I returned to ordinary consciousness.

26 May 1997

In thinking over the incredible scene I had witnessed yesterday, I could not help feeling that it had been staged for my benefit. I asked the Guides to explain what I had witnessed.

'What you saw yesterday was your own field of consciousness. You were viewing your own consciousness. As you know by now, energy is colour. The red you saw was anger, ambition and desire; the green, love, compassion and harmony. The bubbles of blue and the streaks of other colours were ideas and feelings that surface from moment to moment in consciousness. Your field of consciousness is in constant motion; it never rests. Even during sleep, its movement continues at both subconscious and unconscious levels. Contemplate this: Your field of consciousness, and those of all human beings, came into existence millions of years ago, and will continue to be in existence for millions of years to come. Consciousness is eternal.'

Experiments with Psychic Power

As I have mentioned, over a period of years, I conducted many experiments with psychic power for the express purpose of financial gain. At first, I used the psychic faculty to forecast the winners of horse and greyhound races, and shortly after the National Lottery came into being, I incorporated the Lotto draw into my research.

First, let me explain my modus operandi. Switching on, or "opening," the psychic faculty entailed practising certain techniques for about two hours a day over an initial three day period. Usually, on the fourth day, the psychic faculty became operable, and this was heralded during practice by a tingling, or vibrating, between the eyebrows and a repetitive clicking in the left ear. These "symptoms" did not last long; they were simply a sign that the psychic centre, the "Third Eye," was open and in operation.

Through trial and error, I discovered that when this faculty was at its peak, it could, and did, produce the winners of one race after another. But, even with rigorous practice, it did not always perform so admirably. It seemed that when doubt or fear of losing money were present in the mind, then the faculty failed to work. Later on, I discovered that the presence of these two elements – doubt and fear – caused me to try harder, and it was the act of trying too hard that nullified the power to predict accurately.

And so, I tried a different tack. I confined my bet to the first race of each day. This, too, worked successfully for a period of time. The longest successful run of wins was six days in succession, Monday to Saturday. I found that in order to sustain accuracy the practices had to be kept up each day, and this was sometimes easier said than done. If I missed practice on a particular day, for one reason or another, the faculty began to "close," resulting in financial loss the day after. I noticed, too, that on a daily basis, when I backed horses, the faculty worked on horse races; when I backed dogs, it worked on dogs. But, switching between the two was not always successful. For example, if I bet on the first greyhound race of the day, and the first horse race of the day, it would produce the winner of one or the other; seldom did it come up with the winner of both, except during rare "peak times." I also applied this system to forecasts and tricasts in greyhound racing – again with a satisfactory degree of success.

But over a period of time, my wife and I began to notice something "odd" about the money won using this method. I must point out, that because I bet with modest stakes, winnings were proportionately small. Still, "something" always came along to claim the winnings. For example, on the day of a reasonable win, someone would call around unexpectedly and invite us to accompany them for dinner or drinks, thereby usurping the day's profits. Sometimes,

63

within twelve hours of winning, an electrical appliance would break down and have to be replaced. Without fail, the money was always sucked from our grasp, so much so, that we referred to it as "fairy gold." At this point in time, I suspected that there was a force in operation in this matter that was greater than myself. I dubbed this the "Third Force."

In the early days of using the psychic faculty to predict the Lotto results, I did have successes that could be rated "above chance." In the course of three months, I had four match fours. I also had more of these small successes scattered over the following five or six years. But that, it seems, was as high as the Third Force would allow me to go. I was not destined to win serious money.

For instance, one Saturday I had psychically selected numbers for the Lotto draw later that evening. Just as I was about to leave the house to enter the numbers in the draw, an unexpected visitor arrived, delaying me for more than half-an-hour. As soon as he had left, I ran to the nearest Lotto agent's and arrived there ten minutes before the National Lottery computer system closed down prior to the draw. A queue of two or three people stood before me at the Lotto machine. Within minutes, they had been served, and I handed over my play-slip with its eight entries. The shop assistant inserted the play-slip into the machine; it was accepted, and the machine started to print the official Lotto ticket. Then something went wrong. After printing two lines, the machine stopped dead. Even though the numbers I had selected on the six remaining play-slip panels were clearly and heavily marked with a black biro, the machine refused to recognise and register those numbers. Repeated efforts were made by the shop assistant to issue me with a full Lotto ticket but, unfortunately, it was not meant to be. What I ended up with was a ticket that registered the first two sets of numbers only. As it happened, one of those sets of numbers contained a match four; but, on one of the panels refused by the machine were the six winning jackpot numbers.

This was not the only incident where my attempts to win the Lotto jackpot were thwarted. One Saturday afternoon, I lay on the bed either to meditate or astral travel. I fell asleep for three or four minutes, had a dream, and woke up. I dreamt that I had won half-a-million pounds on the Lotto draw later that evening. I remembered that the winning numbers were those I had psychically selected and played in the last mid-week draw. I was not exactly startled or excited by the message of the dream, but decided that I would play the same numbers I had played in the last draw, just in case. Before I could make it to the store, we had a visitor, and I forgot all about the draw. Had I played the Lotto that Saturday as planned, I would now be a wealthier person: the six numbers I would have played were drawn.

In the early days of my experiments, I read somewhere that psychic power was not to be used for personal gain. There was no reason given, and I rationalised that this piece of advice was perhaps designed to keep the "common man" from using it.

Time and time again, from the end of 1992 onwards, I asked the Guides if there was any reason why I should not use psychic power for my own benefit. Their answers were either evasive or vague. For example, a number of times, they said that there were forces within myself that had to be harmonised before I could win large amounts of money. It was implicitly suggested by the Guides, that if I worked hard at study and self-development, I would eventually be "allowed" to use psychic power advantageously. With this in mind, I continued my experiments, on and off, during the succeeding years. And, not knowing any differently, I once considered publishing the "miraculous" "how-to" techniques I had devised for winning money. But the Third Force soon halted this enterprise.

Around August of 1996, I enquired once again about the use of psychic power. The Guide's answer came as a shock.

'You should not use psychic power to win money,' he said. 'This is not in keeping with your destiny. If your Spirit allowed you to accumulate wealth by using psychic power you would not advance spiritually. You would spend the rest of your life amassing money. This is not the way of the Spirit. If you wish to use psychic power, use it in the service of others.'

I was taken aback by this statement, and remained momentarily silent while I thought of what to say next. I felt deflated and somewhat annoyed.

'But why didn't you tell me this years ago?' I said. 'Why did you let me waste all my time on this project?'

'Your time was not wasted,' the Guide replied calmly. 'Every minute you spent training your mind was useful and purposeful. It brought you to the point you are at today. We knew this. We also knew that if we had advised you about the use or misuse of psychic power in the beginning, you would have given up your meditation practices and the other exercises that served to open your mind. If you had lost interest and stopped, we would not have had the opportunity to communicate with, and guide you. If this were the case, you would have remained as you always were: spiritually dead.

'But we saw that the mind training exercises you practised were crucial to your development. We also knew that, because of your materialistic attitude, you would need a concrete goal to work towards; a spiritual one would have been meaningless to you at the time. We saw how strong your greed for wealth was; it was a force, a motivating force. And that is why we decided not to annul this force by telling you the blunt truth about psychic power. The power of your own greed has carried you through this particular stage of your development.

'But now it is time to let go of all thoughts of winning money. Money will not raise your level of consciousness. Only you can do this through your own determination and effort. You can have all the money in the world, but if your consciousness remains narrow and static, what is the use of having money? Money can buy knowledge and information, but it cannot buy enlightenment and wisdom. Neither can it buy inner harmony, happiness or contentment.

Each day you wake up, thank God for what you have and forget what you do not have. Dwelling on things you do not have is not only a waste of precious energy; it is also an illusion.

'Therefore, you must let go of all thoughts of using psychic power for gain. You have played around with psychic power for long enough; you know all you need to know about it – now let it go.'

I remembered the times when the Guides had intimated that when certain forces within myself had been harmonised, I would then be allowed to win big money. Now it was going through my mind that the Guides had lied to me.

'We did not lie to you,' the Guide said, in answer to my thoughts. 'What we said was true. You misinterpreted what we said, as we knew you would. That is why we said it. The "forces" within you that we referred to are greed and materialistic ambition. We suggested that harmonising these forces would open the doorway to acquiring money. This is true. When these forces are harmonised, you will reach a state of spirituality, a state of selflessness.'

The Guide stopped talking. I wondered what "spirituality" and "selflessness" had to do with winning the Lotto.

'It has everything to do with it.' he answered. 'When a true state of spirituality is reached, when you have moved into the realm of the True Self, your thoughts and deeds will be directed towards helping those who are worse off than yourself. In other words, you will feel the needs of others more than you will feel your own. At this stage, if you did win a million pounds, you would give it to those in need, without thought or concern for your own welfare. That is what true spirituality is about – helping others, without thought of recognition or reward for yourself.'

I considered what the Guide had said. One part of me felt elated by the idea of helping others; another part of me felt despondent at the thought of giving away a million pounds.

'Now perhaps the true nature of spirituality is becoming clear to you,' the Guide said. 'Perhaps too, you realise you have further to go to reach this destination. Your last thoughts have indicated that you are on the fence. The idea of helping others appeals to you. The idea of helping yourself also appeals to you. You are at a crucial cross-roads, and the point where the roads divide is as sharp as a razor. The right-hand path leads to spiritual realisation; the left-hand path leads to material realisation. The former leads to a life of harmony and bliss; the latter leads to physical death and defeat.

'At this moment you want to be on both paths at the same time, but at your stage of development this is not possible. You must choose which direction you want to travel.

'If you choose the spiritual path, you must learn to think in terms of what you can give to the world, as opposed to what you can take from it. You must also focus on spiritual ideals. Elevate your daily thoughts, feelings and actions to a spiritual level. Make your work a part of your spiritual aspirations, and make your spiritual aspirations a part of your work.'

'And what about psychic power?' I asked. 'You said I should use it in the service of others.'

'Not "should",' he replied. 'I suggested that if you were to use it, it could be used in the service of others. By "service of others" I mean that you can use it in a counselling capacity if someone needs help. But do not use it frivolously as a party-trick, like you have done in the past. Psychic power deserves respect – it is the power of the Soul.'

Meditation and Visualisation

Shortly after the Guide's revelation regarding psychic power, I received another shock.

'You must learn new methods of meditation,' the Guide told me.

Up until now, I had meditated in two different ways. One involved using a "mandala," a circle drawn on a square white card, with a dot in the centre. I would sit in a half-lotus posture, and, while breathing deeply and evenly, contemplate the circle and dot, alternating the focus of attention between both elements. The circle represents eternity: it has no beginning or no end. The dot symbolises the Source from which all things come into being.

The second method of meditation entailed lying prone, relaxing, and while focussing on the breath, visualising a pink rose complete with leaves and stem. In this exercise, I visualised all aspects of the rose: the stem, thorns, leaves and petals. I found that, when using this technique regularly, it was possible to maintain focus on the image for up to twelve minutes without a break in concentration.

'What you have been doing is exercising your power of concentration and visualisation,' the Guide continued. 'This is good. We are not criticising; we simply wish to point out that there is a more effective way of meditating that, from here onwards, will expand your consciousness at a faster rate. The exercises you have used up until now have been a valuable asset. If you had not developed your power of concentration to such a high degree, you would be unable to focus on, or maintain our communication link for any significant length of time. Therefore, what you have accomplished so far is good. But, it is time to move on. You are ready to enter your next stage of development; that is, if you want to. The choice is yours. If you choose to move forward, you must obtain books on meditation – preferably those of Eastern tradition.'

'But can you not tell me these meditation techniques?' I asked, hoping for a short-cut.

'We could. But remember what we have already told you. It is our task to provide information that is not readily available to you. Whenever information is available in books, then you must learn by yourself. It is better that way.'

Following that instruction, within the next couple of weeks, I borrowed two books from the library: one was *The Tibetan Book Of Living And Dying* by Sogyal Rinpoche; the other *Zen Mind Beginners Mind* by Shunryu Suzuki.

From these books, I learned that what the Guides had told me about my own methods of practice was correct. The methods I had been using were far different from those outlined by the aforementioned authors. A distillation of their technique is: to relax, focus the attention on the breath, and calmly observe thoughts as they arise in the mind. The trick is not to force thoughts from the mind, but simply observe those that are there. After a period of regular practice, trains of thought slow down and become disjointed. In other words, a "gap" appears between thoughts. The object of this technique is to observe, and to allow the mind to rest in the gaps between each thought. Apparently, with sustained practice, these gaps widen, creating a "nothingness" between each thought. This nothingness is the synthesis of an "empty mind."

This brief summary is meant to serve only as an example of how the Guides' teachings influenced my own views on meditation methods; it is not a detailed description of the methods themselves. There is far more to meditation in terms of correct breathing techniques and body posture than I have presented here. To anyone who wishes to take up meditation, I recommend reading at least two books on the subject, or alternatively, seeking the guidance of an experienced teacher.

A Reminder from the Spirit

Unfortunately for me, I did not take the Guides' advice regarding the use of psychic power. I felt that after all the work I had put into it, I should at least give it one more try. To leave it alone, as the Guides had instructed, seemed like giving up; I perceived it as failure.

So, in October 1996, I made a renewed effort to put psychic power to the test once and for all. My plan was to bet a fixed amount of money each day and to set aside all profits. I figured that when enough winnings were in the pool, I could then increase my fixed stake until the profits grew even more. I also changed my technique for activating the psychic faculty. As I soon discovered, this was not a wise move.

On the fourth of October, when passing a betting office, I decided to see if the psychic faculty was in operation. After mentally performing my psychic "trick," I "saw" in my mind's eye the numbers ten and one. This had happened before; it was not unusual to "get" two numbers in the same race. From experience, I knew that one of the numbers would be that of the winner. So, because of the long odds on these two horses, I placed an each-way bet on both. One horse was 25/1, the other 11/1.

The race got under way and I sat to watch the action on screen. Coming into the final furlong, both horses I had bet on struck the front. In the interest of maximum profit, I wanted the 25/1 shot to finish first, and while watching the two horses run neck and neck I became excited. Too excited, perhaps. Suddenly, above the noise of the commentary, I could hear, within my own ears, the sound of my heart beating. It was like the rapid fire of a machine gun. Next, I was struck by an intense chest pain that spread to my neck, jaws and left ear. It became apparent, at that point, that I was having a heart attack. (As a matter of interest, the 25/1 horse did win the race; the 11/1 shot finished second.)

Within a short period of time, I was, once again, in the same hospital I had been in three-and-a-half years earlier. Not only that, but I was in the same ward, and even in the same bed. In the opposite corner of the ward, a man lay dying of cancer. Three-and-a-half years before, the man who had occupied that same bed had died of the same illness. It was as if nothing had changed.

Six days later, I was discharged from hospital, but my health problems were just beginning. In the weeks and months that followed, I felt as if I were really going to die. My heart rhythm remained erratic most of the time. In a resting state, my pulse was 130 beats per minute one moment, and 55 the next. And every time the rhythm changed, it felt as if the heart were rolling over in my chest. I also experienced stabs of pain and stings in the region of the heart. On top of that, I could not move about much due to intense dizzy spells that bordered on blackouts.

When I awoke each morning, I wondered if I would live until the evening; and each evening, I wondered if I would live until the following morning. One particular evening during a bout of chest pain, I sat monitoring my pulse because it was so weak. A wave of dizziness engulfed me and, at that moment, the heart stopped beating. Just as blackness closed in on me, I experienced an explosion inside my head. I not only heard the explosion, but also saw it as a burst of brilliant white light that filled my entire being. Instantly, my heart started beating again.

Shortly after this incident, I "awoke" one night to find myself standing in front of the bathroom mirror. My wife suddenly appeared at the open bathroom door. 'You had better get back in your body,' she said. 'Your heart is about to stop.' With that, I woke up in ordinary consciousness and checked my pulse. The heart rate was dangerously low – 52 beats a minute. I got up and drank coffee to increase the heartbeat, which, thankfully, it did. The next morning, I asked my wife if she remembered being out-of-body; she had no recollection of the incident.

On another occasion, in November, I listened to the wind dragging dried leaves along the ground outside. There was something deeply disturbing about the sound of the wind: it was mournful, morose and filled with foreboding. It made me feel profoundly uneasy, but I could not rationally explain why. Later, I asked the Guides why the sound of this November wind had such an effect on me.

'It is the last sound you will ever hear in this lifetime,' the Guide told me. 'It [the sound] coincides with the moment of your death. That is why you remember it.'

Prior to this I had asked the Guides the reason for this bout of illness.

'You know the reason,' one of the Guides said. 'You have received another tap from the Spirit – a reminder. You have escaped death twice, but you heard the saying in America: "Three strikes and you are out." This applies to you, so tread cautiously. You know what you have to do in this lifetime. Do it!'

Within a few months, medical tests showed that there was no detectable defect in my heart muscle. I now felt better and could live somewhat normally; yet, the chest pains, irregular rhythm, palpitations and mild dizziness continued on and off.

Around June of 1997, I asked the Guides if I would ever get completely well again. I also wondered what type of treatment, if any, would help.

'We will ask the Spirit Healers to help you,' the Guide told me.

Throughout my association with the Guides, I had never heard "Spirit Healers" mentioned before. I wondered why they had not said anything about these healers when I was seriously ill.

'You never asked,' he said. 'You must ask in order to receive. That is the law.' At that point, I did ask. I asked for the assistance of the Spirit Healers — whoever they were.

Two nights later, I had a projection of consciousness to some other dimension. I was lying on a bench inside a small church. To my left and right were two males in ankle-length white robes. I got an intuitive impression that they were Indian monks. At the foot of the bench stood a Catholic priest. It seemed as if the priest was there specifically to observe the healing techniques used by the Spirit Healers. Psychically, I felt that the priest was also a healer, and that, after the healing session, he and the monks intended to compare notes and discuss various healing methods.

With their arms outstretched, palms downwards, the monks made sweeps above my torso. A stupendous sensation of power moved up and down, from head to toe. I could now see a haze of grey-blue energy emanating from my body. Something like a small sphere of bright energy came out of the heart chakra and entered the visible auric field. The monks, each of them using both hands, directed the energy sphere out towards my left shoulder. The sphere then dissolved, some of its energy running down my left arm, some running back across to my right shoulder. I remember the priest becoming very excited about the energy sphere. When the monks positioned and dissolved it, the priest shouted, 'Yes! That's it!'

The next morning I felt that my health was back to normal. For weeks after this event, I experienced no symptoms whatsoever. But, as the end of July came closer, the palpitations and sporadic chest pain returned. I consulted the Guides, and asked why the healing did not work.

'It did work,' was the reply. 'But you have undone the good that was done. You have allowed stress into your life, and that is the cause of this mild relapse. So do not blame the Spirit Healers. The responsibility is yours. You must structure your working time so that physical and mental stress are kept at bay. As we told you before, life must flow naturally, and you must flow accordingly. If you push life, or if life pushes you, disharmony will follow. Live each day in a calm, easy, relaxed manner. Let whatever happens happen. If you wish to remain well, avoid stress at all costs.'

Astral Analysis

So, what are we to make of all this? Do the astral planes really exist? And if so, where? Does the human soul/spirit inhabit these astral/spirit worlds after physical death?

Let us first discuss the astral planes. To those who "travel" into these dimensions, they are indeed real. They are "worlds" similar to our own. As I have mentioned, the catalyst of my own experiences was a book entitled *Journeys Out Of The Body* by Robert A. Monroe, which I read in 1985. Having lost that particular copy of the book, I recently borrowed a reprinted edition from the library to check its publishing history. Once again, I was drawn into reading it, but this time from a different perspective. This time, I was not a novice enthralled by accounts of strange worlds; I could now identify with, and understand, the author's experiences.

For instance, Mr. Monroe states that from his experiences, there is a certain plane, level, or dimension close to our own world, which is inhabited by crazy people. I, too, once found myself in a dimension filled with crazy people. But, I must add that these people were crazy only by our standards of behaviour. They regarded me as "alien," and who knows, if they were to visit our world, they might consider us "crazy." Nevertheless, I thought the parallel between Mr. Monroe's observations and my own experience, in this instance, was interesting. I realise, too, that this does not make a case for the existence of the astral planes.

This brings us to another point of debate. For years, practitioners and proponents of astral projection have argued about the exact location of the astral planes. Do they exist as dimensions of consciousness within ourselves? Or do they exist as worlds outside ourselves? A week ago, I put this question to my Guides.

'Think of it this way,' said the Guide. 'If you were to connect your computer to the telephone line right now, you would have access to a number of information bases and bulletin boards. Supposing a certain bulletin board in California stores information on your subject of interest. You contact this bulletin board, and download the file of your choice. Where does the information exist? Because of your connection, the information now exists in two places at once. It exists on a mainframe computer in California, and it exists on your own computer here in Ireland. If you were to travel physically, at the speed of thought, to the bulletin board's location in California, you could access the information at that location. If you were to travel back home, at the speed of thought, you could read the information on your own computer screen. If your consciousness were to split, as it sometimes does during projection, you would be aware of reading the information both in California and in

Ireland, at the same time. So it is with the astral planes. The energy frequencies of the astral planes exist outside yourself, and also within yourself. Consciousness can experience the astral worlds on both levels.'

Again, this does not provide us with palpable proof of the existence of the astral planes. All any writer can do is present the facts of his or her experiences and allow the reader to make up his or her own mind.

Something I have not mentioned, up until now, are the unusual phenomena sometimes associated with astral projection. For example, a couple of years before my encounter with the "angel," I had what I thought to be a near-death experience. It happened during a period of great stress, shortly after my grandmother had died. One night, I awoke at the sound of her voice. She was calling to me urgently. Next, my ears were filled with the most awesome sounds I had ever heard. My consciousness interpreted these sounds as roaring winds, the pounding of the ocean on a seashore, buzzing, violins playing, bagpipes wailing and bells ringing, all at once. When these terrifying sounds ceased, I found myself at ceiling level looking down at my physical body. The entire experience lasted a number of seconds. It was frightening enough to make me think I was going through the process of dying. In retrospect, however, I now know that this incident was also an out-of-body experience. Recently, I read a book called *Eckankar* by Paul Twitchell. This book deals with the art of soul travel, and on page 149, Mr. Twitchell identifies these sounds as the sounds of "various planes." In my travels on this earth, I have met others who have heard these same sounds at some point in their lives. Thankfully, I have only had this experience once.

Other phenomena associated with astral travel are the bruises sometimes left on the physical body following a skirmish with spirit beings. On occasions when I was attacked, I awoke from the altered state, or sleep, with marks, swelling or soreness on various parts of the body. One time, after a run-in with the spirit of a person I had known well, I awoke in the morning with a blackened, swollen eye. Another morning, when I removed my tee-shirt to wash myself, I was astounded by the sight of cat's claw marks that had torn the skin all along my left shoulder and down my upper arm. I knew by looking at these evenly spaced, thin, scratch lines that I could not have caused them myself. And we did not have a cat at the time.

This leads us to examine the "spirit world." Is there life after physical death? Do the astral worlds play host to the discarnate spirits of animals and humans? From my own experiences over the past eighteen years, I have to answer "yes" to that question.

I once consulted a medium in London, and shortly after she had begun her reading, she announced that a friend of mine, who was "in spirit," wished to communicate with me. She told me the man's name, but I did not know anyone of that name who had died. She then communicated the man's nickname. Again, as far as I was concerned, the man I knew by that name was very much alive. She relayed the message of how this particular person – the one who was "speaking" to her – had passed over. And, I must say, the circumstances of his death were anything but ordinary. Because I believed my friend to be living, I failed to make any connection between him and the "spirit" communicating through the medium. However, about three weeks later, I learned that my friend had died while I was out of the country. Not only that, but the detailed circumstances of his death were exactly as the medium had described.

It has been suggested that mediumship is merely a glorified form of telepathy. Certainly not in this case. I had no knowledge whatsoever of my friend's death when I consulted the medium.

I, too, have a propensity to mediumship, but it is not a faculty I care to exercise. To be quite honest, I am a little scared of it. This apprehension stems from an experiment in 1984 when the spirit of a German doctor entered my field of consciousness. He said that he wanted to continue his healing work through me, and that he would guide me in this matter. To test the validity of this statement, I asked if he could show me how to fix a vertebrae that was out of place in my wife's back. This he did. He "told" me exactly where the vertebrae was located, and how to put it in place. While under the doctor's partial influence, it seemed I knew precisely what to do. But, when the good doctor was supposed to leave, he refused to do so, saying that he wanted to stay and work through me. It took something like four to six hours to get rid of him, and during that period of time his thoughts and feelings constantly intruded on my own consciousness.

After this disturbing incident, I swore I would never again allow the spirit of a deceased person to "communicate" with me. On the rare occasion, if I were contacted by the spirit of someone I knew well, I would listen to what they had to say, then quickly close off. I realise too, that the Guides are spirits of monks who had once lived on earth, but I have always felt that these beings are of a higher order, and therefore, not troublesome or threatening.

Within the past year, I read of the untimely death of a young woman. Her death was sudden and not from natural causes. I knew of this woman because of her career, but did not know her personally. I had never met her. Yet, a couple of hours after reading the news item, and during an altered state of consciousness, the woman "came through" to me. Her message was short and simple: she named the person responsible for her death. When I returned to ordinary consciousness, I was shocked by the "reality" of my meeting with this woman. It was as if she had visited the bedroom where I lay; there was a tremendous sense of "presence" in the room; it was filled with an ineffable feeling of harmony and love.

A few days later, while meditating, I spontaneously entered an altered state of consciousness and met this woman again.

I found myself walking through a cobble-stoned village square, where a festival of some kind was taking place – the words "Mardi Gras" came into my mind. People packed the square; they danced around full of laughter and merriment. I made my way through the crowd towards a vacant bench at the outer edge of the square. The bench was situated close to a stone-built, draw well. As I approached the bench with the intention of sitting down, the woman who had contacted me, accompanied by a blond-haired girl, came running up to the bench with the obvious intention of sitting down. Both were high-spirited and laughing. Just as they reached the bench, the woman caught sight of me and did a double take. 'Michael! It's so good to see you. I'm glad you're here for the festival.'

The woman was obviously overjoyed. "Thrilled to bits" would be a better description. We shook hands and, as our hands clasped, a surge of energy passed through me. I felt myself being filled with love – universal love. We both stood for a few moments, saying how great it was for us to meet in this way. She said we were really fortunate to bump into each other in such a big crowd.

I then remembered the message she had passed on to me a few days be-forehand. I felt slightly guilty because I had not acted on the information. 'Oh, don't worry about that,' she said. 'That'll work itself out in the end. The main thing is to enjoy the festival.'

I then felt tired and confused. I wondered what I was doing, and why I was at the festival. The woman and her friend wanted me to go somewhere with them, somewhere an event was taking place. I said I did not want to go because I was too tired. At that, I returned to ordinary consciousness.

Perhaps the most astounding aspect of this episode is the tremendous feel-ing of universal love that I experienced. As Guides had told me, long before this incident, "universal love" is a profound love for, and affinity with, all living things – not only on this plane of existence, but throughout the universe. This feeling stayed with me for three days, decreasing in intensity with the passing of each day. Why I received this "gift" of love I shall never know. I had no emotional connection whatsoever with the woman in question; as I have said, I did not even know her. As a matter of interest, the initial message given to me by this woman has been proved correct at the time of writing. Even so, this is not hard scientific evidence of an afterlife; it simply reinforces my own personal beliefs in such matters.

Finally, we come to the question of good and bad in the spirit world. We know that most established religions acknowledge the existence of a heaven filled with deities, choirs of angels, saints and souls. We also know that these same religions tell us of devils, demons and such. Do "bad" spirits exist? To that I must answer "yes." But negative forces need a negative environment in which to manifest. The "environment" I speak of is the human mind. A mind that engrosses itself in negativity and morbidity, a consciousness that indulges in feelings of hatred, anger, spite, and so on, is a playground for negative forces. Like attracts like.

All in all, my own experiences have shown me that there is far more good in the spirit world than there is bad. As my Guide once told me, 'When you look at the world around you, you will see two things — ugliness and beauty. If you focus on the ugliness, all you will see is ugliness. If you focus on the beauty, all you will see is beauty. Therefore, you must learn to look for the beauty in everything and everyone you see.'

BOOK II

The Teachings

The Nature of God

In answer to a question about the astral planes, the Guide replied, 'Before you can understand the nature of what you call "the astral planes," it is necessary to know something about the energy structure of the Cosmos. In gaining an understanding of the Cosmos you will be better equipped to understand the nature of God.

'Imagine a giant amphitheatre. It has a central arena surrounded by seven levels constructed of giant blocks of stone. On each of the seven levels there are seven tiers. A perimeter wall encircles the entire construction. In the centre of the central arena there are two trumpeters standing back to back. The trumpets they carry are different: one is black and the other is white. The trumpeters decide to make a sound; one plays a high note, the other plays a low note. The result is discordant; the trumpeters do not like it, so they decide to harmonise the sound they make. The trumpeter who played the high note plays a lower note, and the trumpeter who played the low note plays a higher note. After a number of trials they both produce the same note. The result is harmony. When they started out, each trumpeter made a different sound; there were two sounds to be heard. Now there is one sound. The amphitheatre now contains three elements: the two sound producers and the sound.

'When the sound leaves the trumpets, it fills the amphitheatre. To do so it must travel through the seven levels of the building, occupying each tier and each level in turn. When the sound reaches the outer wall, it bounces off the wall and returns, via the seven levels, to the ears of the trumpeters. By listening to the sound they create, each trumpeter can maintain the exact note that he produces. In this way, the *one* sound is sustained and harmony prevails.

'Imagine what it would be like if you were in the amphitheatre listening to the sound produced by the trumpeters. In the central arena the sound is loud and melodious, but as you move away from the centre through each of the seven levels, you will hear the sound differently at each level. The sound, at each level, will lose some of the integrity it possessed at its point of origin.

'Now, let us compare the Cosmos with the amphitheatre. In the Cosmos there is also a central arena. This is what we [Guides] call the "Central Sphere." Spiritual teachers, masters, angels and saints in the astral dimensions refer to the Central Sphere as the "God-Realm."

'The Central Sphere is an energy plane of pure harmony. It is composed of three energy dimensions, but before we discuss the third energy dimension, let us deal with the two primary energies of the Central Sphere.

'In our analogous amphitheatre we started out with two trumpeters. The two trumpeters are both human beings, and in this regard we can say that they are both of the same species. Yet they are different. Each is an individual with

81

a distinct uniqueness. Also, the trumpets they use to produce the sound are different: one is black, the other is white. And although the trumpets are different in colour, each can produce the same sound. So it is with the primary energies of the Central Sphere: each one is distinctly different; each one is the opposite of the other; yet both work together in perfect harmony, perfect equilibrium.

'But this equilibrium is not passive. As in the case of the trumpeters, a certain amount of tension is required on the part of each individual before they sound their trumpets. If each trumpeter remains passive, nothing will happen. This is how it is with the two Cosmic primary energies. Their contrasting natures create a tension – a tension that produces a third force.

'The third Cosmic force of the Central Sphere can be likened to the sound produced by the trumpeters. It is a force of pure harmony. It flows from its dual creators and carries the qualities of each creator. The sound in the amphitheatre originated from both a black and a white trumpet, and as we now know, the note from each trumpet blended to create the same sound. So it is with the third force of the Central Sphere: it is individual; it is one, and although it is one, it is maintained by, and possesses, the contrasting qualities of *two*.

'Now that the triple energies and the trinal unity of the Central Sphere are clear to you, from here on we will refer to the energy of the Central Sphere as "Divine Energy."

'Divine Energy is not only an energy composed of dual qualities, but it is also consciousness: it has a purpose, a specific intent. It is the thought-form behind all creation. The trumpeters in our analogy started out by playing two different notes [one high, one low], but they both wanted to sound the same note, which they eventually did. Therefore, each trumpeter had the same intent. The harmonious sound that they ultimately produced was the *intent* of its creators. Divine Energy also inherits its intent from its source of origin. That intent, or purpose, is to evolve creation and to maintain the equilibrium of that creation.

'In order to achieve its objective, Divine Energy cannot stay in the Central Sphere. Like the sound of the trumpets filling the whole amphitheatre, Divine Energy permeates all quarters of the Cosmos. Divine Energy manifests in many ways: it maintains your "clockwork universe"; it manifests on earth as the "work of nature"; and at a human level, it is the power behind miracles.

'Like the sound of the trumpets in the amphitheatre, Divine Energy is at its loudest and purest in the Central Sphere. Here it is an harmonious, high-frequency energy. But as I have said, because of its intent it cannot remain in this state, and is compelled, by its intent, to pass through, and maintain, the seven Cosmic layers of energy, before it takes form in the eighth.

'These seven Cosmic layers of energy are established wavelengths of energy; they are known to you as the "astral planes." In order to understand the structure of the astral energy planes, think of each plane as a note on a musical scale. Each plane has a different wavelength and the frequency of each wave-length ranges from high to low, making each plane denser than the one "above" it.

'Each particular plane is perceived by consciousness as a "world," and each is composed of energy frequencies that are perceived by consciousness as "geographical locations," such as continents, countries, counties and so forth.

'As Divine Energy flows through each plane, it carries out the necessary checks and balances to maintain the energy states of that plane. This process can be likened to the flow of blood in the human body. As blood is pumped around the body it carries oxygen and nutrients to nourish and sustain body cells and tissue. In much the same way, the Divine Energy nourishes and sustains the existence of the Cosmos. Not only that, but it also incessantly strives to create new life-sustaining planets throughout the universe, so that life and consciousness, as you know it, will never cease to exist and evolve.

'From what I have told you so far, you now understand that the Cosmos is a conflux of energy wavelengths; it is a powerhouse of energy. All that you see around you is energy; the planet, trees, flowers, plants, animals and human beings are all energy.

'As we have said, Divine Energy is not just energy but is also conscious-ness. All energy is consciousness in one way or another. Think about this carefully. On your planet each insect, each plant, each human being is a unit of energy. But it is also a unit of consciousness. There are many different degrees of consciousness, ranging from the rudimentary consciousness of molecules to the more sophisticated consciousness of human beings. This means that every-thing possesses an awareness of its existence – a consciousness. Energy is con-sciousness: consciousness is energy. For this reason, the whole of creation, including all that your planet contains, could be described as a "stream of con-sciousness."

'Once again, we must return to the amphitheatre. In our example we saw how the sound, once it had left the trumpets in the central arena, travelled outwards to fill the whole building. We also saw how this same sound re-turned to the ears of the trumpeters, helping both of them to maintain the exact note that they produced. Divine Energy functions in the same fashion. Its energy flows out from the Central Sphere and returns to the Central Sphere, thus completing an energy circuit.

'But as I have said, this energy is not just energy; it is also consciousness. And as we have seen, the purpose of Divine Energy is to evolve consciousness. In order to achieve this, it must travel to and inhabit the plane of matter, the earth plane. The plane of matter is the principal learning field; this means that consciousness must occupy the planet, Earth, in order to grow. Once a unit of consciousness has learned all it can learn on one arc of universal evolution, it will make its way back to the Central Sphere, bringing with it all it has learned. It will reside there until the dawning of the next phase of evolution, and then it will travel "down" the planes and "descend" once again into the plane of matter.

'This does not mean that units of energy/consciousness like the human Soul/Spirit return to the Central Sphere at the end of one lifetime on earth. It may take a million years for the universe to progress through one arc of evolution. For the individual unit of energy and consciousness, this means living innumerable existences in various material forms. Also, the return journey to the Central Sphere is not exclusively a conscious choice. When a certain level of evolution is reached, the unit of consciousness responds to the natural pull, the inflow, of the Central Sphere.

'A point to note is that the outflow and inflow of Divine Energy creates a pull and push effect throughout the entire Cosmos, which gives rise to a "Cosmic tide." This tide governs the whole of creation; for example, growth and decay, plenty and scarce, construction and destruction.

'Also, I must point out that when I speak of "units of energy and consciousness," I am not implying that all units are separate from each other. On a material level, they are; on an energy level, they are not. All living things, all sentient beings are connected to each other by a fine thread of energy. This explains why the mind of one individual can sometimes know what is in the mind of another, regardless of the distance between them. It explains, too, why some evolved animals can "sense" a human's feelings and intent. Not only are all sentient beings connected to each other by way of energy, but each is also linked to the Central Sphere by a silver-white thread. Again, this connection is one of both energy and consciousness, and it enables the Creator to be conscious of all that is created. In other words, the Creator, God, is conscious of Himself through the collective consciousness of His creation. In this way, God is all and all is God.

The Soul/Spirit

During my school-days, religious education laid emphasis on the soul, but there was not much said about the spirit. To my mind the spirit was something that existed on a far higher plane; it was something remote and largely inaccessible. First-hand experience of the spirit seemed to be reserved for biblical characters, and not at all for the common man. I had also learned that when the physical body's life expired, the soul left the body and went to another "place", there was little mention of a spirit in this process. Yet when people in the community spoke of the appearance of a discarnate entity (ghost), the apparition was usually referred to as a "spirit," not a "soul." I often wondered about this: Were the soul and spirit two different entities, or were the words "soul" and "spirit" used interchangeably to describe one state of being.

In the course of the Guides' teachings, they used the word "Spirit" (with a capital 'S') to describe the spiritual aspect of sentient beings. And when they spoke of this spiritual aspect on a Cosmic level, they used the term "Soul/Spirit." I asked the Guide what the difference was, if any, between the two.

'You know that the whole of creation is composed of energy. The Soul/Spirit is also energy. It cannot be anything else. So let us begin by saying that the Soul and Spirit are two different aspects of one energy. In this regard, the Soul/Spirit is a replica of the Central Sphere; it is a microcosm of the macrocosm. This is not surprising since the Soul/Spirit is conceived in the Central Sphere.

'The Central Sphere is the origin of all energy. In a previous discussion we spoke of this energy as "Divine Energy." It is like a pool of living, white light. A seething mass of tiny, brilliant white sparks comprise this pool of light. But the sparks are not separate; they are all connected by silver-white threads of energy. Each spark is either a Soul/Spirit or a potential Soul/Spirit, depending on the phase of evolution it is at. Some sparks could be described as "infants" simply because they are newly "born" and have not developed consciousness as you know it. Yet, each created spark, regardless of its evolutionary level, carries the intent of its Creator. As you will remember from our discussion on the Cosmic energy structure, there are two aspects to this One intent; that is, to evolve consciousness and to maintain Cosmic balance. The dual aspects of this One intent give rise to the same dual aspects in an energy spark. The expression of these aspects are, what you call, "Soul" and "Spirit." I will explain this more fully further on; for now, we will talk about how an energy spark develops its potential to become a human Soul/Spirit.

'In order for you to understand what I am about to say, you will need a framework of reference.'

From behind his back, the Guide produced a sheet of yellowed parchment, about A5 in size, and held it in front of my eyes.

'Read this,' he said. 'Read it, and memorise it.'

When I focussed on the sheet of paper, I saw that it contained the following text:

1. First Plane   — Intent (The Central Sphere)

2. Second Plane   — Awareness

3. Third Plane   — Consciousness

4. Fourth Plane   — Harmony

5. Fifth Plane   — Feeling [Emotion]

6. Sixth Plane   — Energy [Creative]

7. Seventh Plane   — Being

8. Eighth Plane   — Experience [i.e., experiencing the world of matter through the five physical senses. The world of matter is the earth plane, with its four elements: Earth, Air, Fire and Water.]

Once I had read, and reread, the script-like text, the Guide continued. 'Now let us examine how an energy spark becomes a human Soul/Spirit.

'In order to evolve, the spark must pass through seven energy planes of non-matter and ultimately inhabit the eighth plane — the world of matter, the plane of Experience. It is at this level, through experience, that the potentials of the seven non-material energy planes will be developed. I must point out that although each of the eight, energy planes exist independently, they are interconnected and interactive.

'The energy spark begins its journey in the Central Sphere, the plane of Intent. Here, it becomes aware of its purpose, and although that purpose is dual, it is One. Here, there is no conflict of interest between each aspect of the spark's purpose; therefore, all that exists on this plane does so in a state of harmony. But the spark cannot exist at this level forever. Motivated by the nature of its intent, it flows out of the Central Sphere carried on a current of Divine Energy.

'On its outward journey, the spark travels to the second plane, the plane of Awareness. This is not a sensory awareness; it is what could be described as "psychic" awareness. When the spark assimilates the energy vibration of Awareness, it does not become instantly aware of everything in the Cosmos, but simply develops the potential for awareness. In other words, the seed is sown. And that seed, like any other, has to grow.

'So it moves on. It enters the plane of Consciousness. Again, the frequency of this plane affords only the potential for consciousness.

'In the fourth plane there is harmony. When the spark adopts the vibration rate of this plane, the attributes of the "upper" planes become harmonized in the spark. It now has intent, the capacity for both awareness and consciousness, and the potential to harmonize the attributes of the "upper" and "lower" planes.

'The fifth energy plane endows the spark with the potential for feeling. When awareness, consciousness, and harmony are developed to a certain level, the spark will have the potential to experience emotions.

'The energy of the sixth plane is primarily creative. When an adequate degree of awareness, consciousness and feeling are developed, the spark, through the energy of the sixth plane, will have the potential to create; the potential to become a more sophisticated unit of energy and consciousness. Again, the energy is only a potential in the spark until it develops a greater degree of awareness, consciousness and feeling.

'The seventh energy plane is the plane of Being. Here, energy has the potential to take form. The spark, with seven energy frequencies now absorbed, has the capacity to develop an energy system, and ultimately, a complex energy form. The energies of this plane are what could be called "universal stuff." They are the forces that form all matter. An example of a complex energy form would be the human energy system, namely, the aura with its seven primary chakras.

'The eighth plane, the planet, Earth, is the plane of Experience. All life forms, at this level, are vehicles for energy, consciousness and experience. This is where the spark will evolve through the experiences of many physical incarnations. Once it reaches a certain level of evolution, it experiences the world of matter through the five senses of a physical body, be it animal or human. And, as the spark evolves, so does the expression of its intent – the Soul/Spirit.

The Guide fell silent, giving me the opportunity to ask a question I had in mind: 'The seven non-material levels that the spark passes through – are these the astral planes?'

'In a sense, yes. They are the seven energy wavelengths of the astral planes. Once the spark has absorbed all seven wavelengths, or vibration rates, it becomes a replica of the Cosmos; in this way, each part contains an image of the whole.'

I was still not too clear on the nature of the energy wavelengths. The Guide sensed this and explained.

'For the sake of simplicity,' he said, 'think of these energy vibration rates in terms of colour. Relate it to the seven energy chakras of the human system. The spark in the Central Sphere is brilliant white. It is connected to the Central Sphere by a white thread of energy: a thread so brilliantly white that it looks like silver. When the spark travels to the second plane, it picks up the colour violet. This colour is now contained in both the spark and the white thread. It then moves on to the next plane and absorbs the colour blue; the next plane, green; the next, yellow; the next, orange; and finally, red. Now the spark and the white thread consist of all seven colours. But, as I have said, these vibration rates are only potentials in each spark until they become fully developed.'

'What do you mean by "potentials"?' I asked.

'Think of the eight levels as eight countries. Each country has its own language. An individual from the first country visits each of the other seven countries in turn. The individual does not know the language of each country, but by being in a particular country he is given the opportunity to learn the language. In other words, being in the country enhances his potential to learn the language.

'But let us move on. Let us look at how the Soul/Spirit functions on the earth plane. Let us see how the Soul/Spirit expresses its intent.

'The Soul is the psyche of each human being. It is what you call "the subconscious mind." The Soul carries out the intent to evolve consciousness; it does this by absorbing knowledge. It receives its information through the five physical senses, and works in tandem with the Ego-mind. It records, and stores, the memory and all the experiences of each lifetime. But the Soul can also access information at the level of Awareness; this attribute of the Soul is known to you as "psychic power."

'The Spirit could be referred to as the "unconscious" mind. Unlike the subconscious, it is not readily accessible to consciousness. Its intent is to strive towards balance. It continually refers to the experiential memories of the Soul and decides what experiences are necessary to maintain a balance on the individual's evolutionary journey. For example, if the individual is wealthy in one lifetime, it may be necessary to experience poverty in the next. This is how balance is maintained. On a mundane level, the Spirit has the power to heal; this it does by rebalancing the individual's energy system.

'Spirit and Soul could be likened to a student and his textbook. Let us say that the Spirit is the student, and the Soul is the textbook. The student knows what he has to learn in order to fulfil his ambition. He learns from reading the textbook, and as he studies each chapter, his knowledge expands. Let us say that he is half-way through the book. By referring occasionally to the chapters he has studied, he reminds himself of what he has learned. And by glancing at the chapters that he has not read, he sees what needs to be learned.

'The Soul and Spirit combined are like a two-way mirror: Spirit reflects heaven, and Soul reflects earth. Also, on a Cosmic level, you could also say that the Spirit is an architect, and the Soul is a builder. If both work in harmony, then they are capable of producing a great edifice; but if a conflict of interest occurs, Soul and Spirit lose their natural unity of expression, and discord results throughout the whole being.'

I tried to imagine how a conflict of interest could occur in the Soul/Spirit.

'This will become clear through further discussions. Suffice it to say, the fault lies in the human Ego-mind.'

The Essence of God

I contemplated the eight Cosmic planes of existence, trying to visualise how they would look. The mental image I conjured up was one of a circle surrounded by seven concentric circles. I wondered where the innermost circle, the Central Sphere, might be situated, relative to the universe. When I asked the Guide, he replied with another question.

'Where is Divine Energy located?'

After a moment of thought, I answered, 'Divine Energy must be everywhere.'

'Then, that is your answer,' the Guide said. 'All energy "worlds," all energy wavelengths, co-exist with your own universe. These "worlds" are right beside you; their frequencies are within you.'

The Guide paused to let that piece of information sink in. When I tried to analyse it, I became more confused. The words "The Kingdom of Heaven is at hand . . ." flashed into my mind.

'If you want to find the harmony of the Central Sphere,' he continued, 'if you want to find Divine Energy, look no further than your own heart. Within yourself, the most obvious expression of Divine Energy is love. Love is the Essence of God. But love is not simply an emotional feeling: it is an energy – a particular frequency of energy that manifests in different ways.

'The energy frequency called "love" has an innate duality: it is both attractive and expansive. It has the power to pull, and hold, units of energy/consciousness together, as in family units. It also has the power to expand family units. Take an average human couple. The male and female are drawn together by feelings of love; they become bound to each other by love; they unite in love, and because of their union the family unit expands, its numbers increase. When male and female feel love as an emotion, and express that love, they are, in fact, responding to a particular frequency of energy. All living things, in a predetermined way, respond to the energy called "love." By the power of love, vehicles [physical bodies] for energy/consciousness are created in your world. Without this energy, there would be neither creation nor cohesion.'

On hearing the Guide's last statement, the words "propagation of the species" sprang to mind. It made me wonder if insects, fish, birds and animals experienced the feeling of love.

The Guide, reading my thoughts, said, 'They do. They feel the energy of love, but that is not a feeling of being "in love." To these beings, love is experienced as an attraction towards the conditions for propagation and as a compulsion to propagate.

'In human beings the energy of love is felt as an emotion, but it operates at different energy levels for different purposes. When love operates through the lower Base and Sacral chakras, it is sexual love: a feeling that attracts one individual to another and compels the individuals to engage in the act of procreation. When it functions through the Solar Plexus and Heart chakras, it is love of family, friends and humanity in general.

'But for the individual and the world at large, the most profound love is "Universal Love." When attuned to this energy, it is experienced by the individual as a feeling of love for all living things. It bestows a sense of unity, harmony and affinity with *all*, hence the name, Universal Love.'

I asked the Guide if there were a special technique for attuning oneself to and experiencing Universal Love.

'Yes,' he answered. 'You must practice loving. This means that you must create the conditions within you whereby Universal Love can exist. By practising loving regularly, the corresponding energy frequency in your own being will link into the frequency of Universal Love. It is similar to tuning your radio to a certain frequency and receiving what is being broadcast on that frequency. Although you may hear what is being broadcast in your own home, the broadcast itself is not within your home; it may be miles away. In a similar way you can attune yourself to the energy frequency of Universal Love.

'The first prerequisite is self-love. By that, I do not mean that you must become selfish. Loving yourself means respecting and looking after yourself, on all levels of being. Treat your body as if it were a small baby. For instance, you would not fill a baby's lungs with cigarette smoke day after day. You would not fill a baby's stomach with alcoholic drinks. You would not clog a baby's system with fatty, unwholesome foods. You would not condemn your child to working long hours in an unhealthy environment. And so it should be with your body: treat it properly with wholesome food, exercise and balanced work practices; give yourself the gift of regular meditation to calm the mind and emotions; make time in your day for silence and for contemplating spiritual matters – these practices will open your being to the flow of Divine Energy that I refer to here as Universal Love.

'Also, you must love life. Love each day and each minute of each day. Yes, life can be lived and loved. There is no reason why life should be a miserable affair. If you do not like some aspect of your life – change it! Get rid of all sources of worry, annoyance, pettiness, aggravation, strife and so forth. If you allow these things to rule your life, then they will rob you of the capacity to love the life that God gave you.

'The next step is to love all that is within nature, for nature is the expression of God. And for those who seem to think differently, "all that is within nature" includes the environment. All creatures are God's creatures, regardless of whether or not all creatures please mankind. Some individuals may say: "I hate snakes", or "I hate rats and mice", or "I hate the insects that eat crops grown for human consumption." Remove the word "hate" from your vocabulary. There is no advantage in hating any living creature. All living creatures have their own place of importance in the scheme of things. And always bear in mind that each tree and leaf are God's tree and leaf; each blade of grass is God's blade of grass; each weed is a plant of God; therefore, when you destroy something within nature, you destroy the work of God. As I have told you, the Creator and the Created are One. So how can you hope to experience the Divine if you participate in the destruction of Creation?

'Learn to love your fellow man. This is achieved by altering your habitual, negative way of thinking. Remove the habit of forming opinions and judgements when you look at other people and the situations they are involved in. Opinions and judgements serve only to make life difficult. From opinions and judgements spring perceptions of right and wrong, good and bad, you and them. These perceptions fuel feelings of dislike, hatred, aversion and hostility. Feelings such as these are unwholesome and unproductive; more often than not, they will drag you into the mire of barbed gossip, criticism and antagonism. And for what? You may be dead tomorrow morning.

'Therefore, it will behove you to nurture the positive qualities of courtesy, consideration, compassion and understanding. When these vital elements are prominent in your consciousness, the energy of your Heart chakra will begin to oscillate, or vibrate, at the same frequency as Universal Love, the Essence of God. Thus a link with the energy frequency of Universal Love is firmly established, and, consequently, the corresponding feelings of unity, harmony, love of all living things, and a joy of living will be experienced in full.'

The Purpose of Life

The Guide's explanation about the Spirit's journey from the Central Sphere to the world of matter revived questions I had carried in my mind for many years. In the past, from a Christian viewpoint, I had often grappled with questions relating to the nature of heaven (paradise) and the purpose of existence on earth. If heaven is such a beautiful place, then why leave it? Why come to earth to toil and suffer all sorts of calamities? In the course of our discussions the Guides had made it clear that the whole purpose of life, as we know it, is to learn – to evolve consciousness. But in thinking of the astral planes, the worlds of energy and beauty, I wondered why we, as spirits, could not conduct our learning at these levels. At least, on the astral planes, we would not have physical suffering to cope with.

I put this question to the Guides; both were present at this discussion.

'As you already know, the principal purpose of life on earth is to expand consciousness. To do this successfully, consciousness must be challenged by experiences; this is the way lessons are learned. And it is only on the earth plane that the full gamut of life's lessons can be experienced first-hand. At this level, life, in all its forms, is an ongoing process of experiencing. Experience is life, and life is experience. Life without experience is lifeless. It is only through *experience* that consciousness can grow.

'But why can't we experience things on the astral planes?' I asked.

The Guide who had addressed me paused a moment before answering. 'Let us begin at the beginning. The astral planes are planes of energy. On the astral planes you construct the world around you (forms) by thinking and feeling. Where is the challenge in that? On earth, if you want to make a clock it is necessary to make each independent part, and then learn how to put those parts together in a way that works correctly. The business of making a clock is a challenge and you learn something from that challenge. But on the astral energy planes if you want a clock you simply think the clock into existence. Not that time-keeping is relevant at these levels.

'Perhaps if we explain how consciousness evolves on earth, this concept will become clear to you. As you now know, the growth of consciousness is the will of God. God is conscious of Himself through His creation; therefore, the more His creation learns and experiences, the more God becomes aware of.

'Let us begin with a simple organism that lives and carries out its function in the soil of the earth. It lives through its existence as an organism, and when its life-span comes to an end, it returns once again to its energy state. But it now contains a memory of its life-span as an organism. It may incarnate as an organism many times over until its conscious awareness expands. Expansion of consciousness is the natural order of things. So once the organism reaches a certain level of consciousness, it will strive to exist on a higher arc and, consequently, its consciousness will incarnate into plant life. Once it reaches the necessary level of consciousness, after numerous existences in the plant kingdom, that unit of consciousness will graduate to the insect kingdom. Through countless incarnations and experiences in the insect world, its consciousness will expand yet again. According to the temperament it has developed, it may decide at this stage to incarnate as a bird or a fish.'

'What do you mean by "according to temperament"?' I asked.

'I mean that once the conscious awareness of an insect becomes sufficiently expanded, flying insects will desire to become birds, and water insects will desire to become creatures of the deep. But, bear in mind, consciousness does not stay at this level; it goes on evolving.

'After millennia of experience in these conditions, the unit of consciousness, now even more expanded, will gravitate towards the animal kingdom. At first, depending on its level of consciousness, it is likely to become an animal of the wild; then a farm animal; then a domestic animal, a pet. It is at this stage that the unit of consciousness is almost human. Through lifetimes of being a pet it learns from its human masters, until it reaches the stage where it is ready to incarnate into human form. Think of the animals you have known who, from an early stage in their lives, exhibited higher intelligence. These animals appear to understand what you are thinking and feeling. Animals who exhibit such qualities are considerably evolved units of consciousness; they are ready for a higher arc of evolution; they are ready to exist in the human form.

'Have you ever wondered why many human beings behave like animals? You know what we mean. You once saw a dog whose belly was full to capacity; he could not eat any more. Although he did not want the meagre scraps of food left in his dish, he guarded the dish with utmost vigilance. When another dog approached the dish, the satiated dog growled and snarled, preparing to fight. And he would have fought; he would have ripped lumps of flesh from his perceived enemy. He would have fought to the death to defend something that he did not even want. Consider how this applies to many human beings. Many humans want to have more than anyone else, even though they do not need what they already have.

Just as the Guide had finished speaking, I suddenly recalled a lucid mental picture of a black and white mongrel standing over an almost-empty, cracked, enamel dish; his teeth were bared in a snarl and the hair stood on the back of his neck. Further away, a coal-black, Labrador pup cowered, retreating reluctantly from his foray. I had witnessed this incident in a farmyard at some point of time in my life. In my mind's eye, I could see the yard clearly, but trying to recall where and when created an uncomfortable itching sensation in my solar plexus. The Guide's voice brought my attention back to the discussion.

'Consider, also, how humans behave in times of war. Think of the carnage, the trauma, the pain and torture they inflict on each other. And for what? Territory and worldly power that they will never be capable of enjoying because of their incessant fears of reprisal, attack and ultimate material loss.

'This is the behaviour of humans whose consciousness is on a lower scale of evolution. It takes many lifetimes in human form for that unit of consciousness to become aware of its true [spiritual] identity and its true purpose. The unit of consciousness evolves instinctively, up to a point. It is driven by its inherent desire, or intent, to exist and evolve. When it reaches a certain point in human evolution, it becomes conscious of the spiritual aspect of itself. In other words, it becomes aware of God and it realises its relationship with God. At this point, the individual knows that he and God are one; he knows that he and his fellow-man are one; and he knows that all living beings are children of God. When consciousness reaches this level, the individual becomes incapable of harm.

'The evolution of consciousness is like a cone-shaped spiral. At the lowest point it is quite narrow; however, at each upward arc the spiral widens. This is how it is with consciousness: as the level of consciousness is raised, it expands. The more it is raised, the more it expands. And the more it expands, the less it rejects and the more it embraces.'

This, to me, seemed a plausible explanation for the purpose of life on earth. If a unit of consciousness had an innate desire, or intent, to expand, to experience ALL, then it would be quite natural for that unit of consciousness to desire physical existence on earth, in one form or another, many times over.

The second Guide took up the discussion where the first left off.

'At this point in evolutionary history, individuals are beginning to break free of outmoded, established ways of thinking. The individual has now developed an appetite for knowledge. There are many ways to acquire knowledge, such as reading, taking courses, listening to talks, lectures, and so on. But knowledge needs to be tempered with wisdom, and wisdom is attained from within. It is attained through self-observation, meditation and contemplation. When both knowledge and wisdom reach a certain level, they merge to create a universal understanding.

'Think of it in this way. You have two glass jars of equal size standing side-by-side; each is capable of holding a gallon of water. Close to the top is a glass tube connecting the two jars. If one jar is half-full of water and the other is two-thirds full, you have two separate quantities of water. If, on the other hand, the level of water is raised to the top of both jars, the water in each will merge via the glass tube. In this way, the water in both jars becomes one. And that is how it is with wisdom and knowledge. They both have to be raised to a certain level before they unite to become wisdom, knowledge and universal understanding.

'How would you define universal understanding?' I inquired.

'Universal understanding is an understanding of the nature of the *whole* self, an understanding of others, an understanding of all living things, and an understanding of the energy and consciousness integrated in the *all*. It is sometimes referred to as "Cosmic consciousness".'

Today, on finishing the discussion relating to the purpose of life, I asked the Guides if there were any other reason why a person should go to the bother of expanding their consciousness, apart from it being the will of God?

'Expansion of consciousness is the singular, most important thing in the life of any individual. You can go through life working all the hours of the day to make money in abundance; you can buy property, and fill your property with all the luxuries you desire; you can purchase land and develop more properties – you can do all these things, but throughout your life if you do not develop yourself, your own consciousness, then you lose an exquisite opportunity. When physical death arrives, all your wealth, all your luxury and all your property will simply disappear. These things have no permanence. The one and only thing that survives physical death is your consciousness. It is eternal and, therefore, it is the only thing that you have of any value.'

Destiny

In thinking about the 'Purpose Of Life', I contemplated what we human beings call "destiny." I asked the Guide how he would define destiny.

'Destiny is the *will* of the Spirit,' he said. 'It is the intent of the individual Soul. From the Spirit's point of view, destiny can be a desire or a number of desires aimed in the same direction. I once said to you that the Spirit is like an architect; it designs the blueprint for the Soul/Spirit's evolutionary journey. But in the course of this journey, the Spirit continuously assesses the Soul/Spirit's progress and revises the blueprint to compensate for imbalances that occur during its individual and collective existences on earth. To put it succinctly, the Spirit engineers the direction of the individual's life, and that direction is aimed at enlightenment. When the Spirit attains enlightenment, it can disengage from the cycle of earthly birth, existence and death. It can then reside on the astral planes and work for the good of humanity, if it so chooses.

'On its journey towards enlightenment, through many incarnations, the Spirit will, more often than not, choose existences, environments and relationships that are most likely to provide the lessons it needs to learn. If the Spirit sees that it needs the solitude of a monastery, then it will be born into a life that has the potential to fulfil that need; if the Spirit wishes to experience hunger, it will be born into poverty or famine; and so on. You may think that human existence is much the same for one as it is another. But give this matter some thought. Contemplate, for example, the disparity in the following lives: the life of a fisherman on a Greek island; the life of a lawyer, and mother of two, in a busy, modern metropolis; the life of a terrorist who devotes his life to armed struggle; the life of a country's president or prime minister; the life of a pop-star; the life of a beggar in any city; the life of a farmer; the life of an artist or writer; the life of a young slave in a sweat-shop. If you give each of these examples some thought, you will realise the diversity of experiences intrinsic in each of these different lives.'

I asked why it took so many lifetimes to reach enlightenment.

'Because the Ego gets in the way. During many of the individual's earth plane existences, the destiny of the Spirit is often diverted by the Ego-mind in residence. The Ego-mind becomes so dominant and wayward that the Spirit's purpose cannot be achieved.'

I could not imagine how this might happen and asked the Guide to explain. He considered his answer for a few moments.

'The main problem is conditioning. More often than not, the Ego-mind of each existence becomes the victim of negative, materialistic conditioning causing the individual to think and act in a certain way. But this developed conditioning may not be compatible with the Spirit's blueprint, its destiny. So the Spirit is faced with the task of changing the individual's consciousness, his way of thinking, and ultimately, his direction in life. This can be a difficult chore.

'Take, for example, an actor in a play. He is cast to play the role of a son in a certain production. In the play he has sisters, brothers, mother, father, uncle, aunt, friends and neighbours. The son, played by the actor, is the central character in the play. So, night after night, the actor dons the character's clothes and proceeds on stage to play the life of the character.

'But before long the character begins to take over the actor's life. Off-stage, without realising it, the actor now walks and talks like the character he plays. He dresses like the character; he has even adopted the character's false notions, false hopes and dreams. As a result of this take-over by the character, the actor has forgotten who he, himself, is. His own personal goals and dreams are now feeble memories. There is nothing left of his own self – his true self. Unwittingly, the actor immersed himself so much in the character, that he actually became the character.

'This is what happens when the Ego-mind takes control of the entire being. The Ego becomes so entrenched in its conditioned, materialistic role that it forgets, and often denies, who it really is. As a result of this anomaly the "voice" of the Spirit cannot be heard; it becomes blocked out. This means that the Spirit cannot communicate with, or guide, the individual. Quite often this separation leads to physical disease, depression, accidents and physical death.'

I remembered my own case when I was near death with pneumonia. Six months beforehand I was told by the Guide that my Spirit was preparing to withdraw (die) because I was not following my destiny at the time. On two other occasions, when I had suffered serious illness, the Guides explained that the conditions were caused by the Spirit in an attempt to "wake me up," to make me see reality, so that I would follow the way of the Spirit, and not the way of the Ego.

I was curious as to how the separation of the Spirit and Ego-mind could cause depression. I asked the Guide.

'It is best to point out that not all cases of depression are caused by the Spirit. As you know, depression can be brought about by an hormonal or chemical imbalance in the body. The depression of which we speak is the type of depression that manifests without any apparent cause.

'This happens when the interests of the Ego and Spirit are in conflict. The Spirit wants to do one thing: the Ego wants to do something else. If the Spirit cannot get its message through, if it cannot get the individual on to the right path, it shrinks its energy; that is, it pulls some of its [spiritual] energy from the individual's field of consciousness. This results in the mental and emotional energy fields being depleted of vital energy, and, subsequently, the individual is plunged into the depths of lassitude and despair.

'Think of this energy depletion in terms of an electric light bulb. When the light bulb receives its full complement of energy, it shines brightly and illuminates all around it. But when the energy supply is notably reduced, the light becomes weak and ineffectual. This is what happens in most cases of depression. In order to avoid bouts of depression recurring, the cause of the depression must be addressed. The individual's link with Spirit must be re-established. As you know, this is accomplished through regular meditation. If the individual wishes to use prayer, before or after meditation, that, too, will help elevate consciousness to a spiritual level. When Ego and Spirit are in close communion, and when the ambition of the Ego is aligned with the destiny of the Spirit, great harmony fills the life of the individual.'

'Can you explain,' I asked, 'how the spirit communicates with the Ego. How is this communication experienced?'

'The Spirit communicates with the individual's Ego-mind through the psyche, or Soul. The Soul is the Spirit's link to the earth plane. The communication of the Spirit is like an inaudible whisper. It is experienced as an urge: an inexplicable desire to do something, be something or achieve something. Take, for instance, a child prodigy who, from an early age, "knows" that his or her life will be devoted to a particular art. In this case, the voice of the Spirit is strong. But it is not so with all individuals. For instance, a plumber might experience an urge to carve stone, but his conditioned Ego-mind tells him that carving stone is not his trade. So he does not attempt to carve stone. He goes on with the plumbing trade he has learned, and, all the while, there is a first-rate talent within him waiting to be expressed. This is how the will, the destiny designed by Spirit, is frustrated.

'Does this mean that destiny and talent are one and the same thing?' I queried.

The Guide replied, 'No. The Spirit, in any one lifetime, will express itself and learn through a certain talent. Or it may seek to master a particular talent during a number of earthly existences.'

He fell silent. I thought back to what he had said about the Spirit causing accidents. 'Are all accidents caused by the Spirit?' I asked.

'No, not always,' he answered. 'Sometimes accidents are engineered by the Spirit in an attempt to change the course of the individual's life. You have read of such accidents.'

This was true. I had read accounts of extreme change taking place in people's lives following serious accidents, illness and near-death experiences. This change quite often brought not only a change of direction, but also a profound sense of purpose to the lives of those concerned.

'That is the work of the Spirit,' he continued. 'The Spirit arranges circumstance so that it can break the power of the Ego. When the power of the Ego is broken, the True Self, the Spirit, can express itself through the individual, and thereby realise its destiny.'

'You mentioned, too, that the Spirit will cause death when a person is not living according to the Spirit's wishes,' I said. 'I cannot understand why the Spirit would do this.'

'You must always bear in mind that, as far as the Spirit is concerned, there is no such thing as death. The Soul/Spirit never dies; therefore, the Spirit is unconcerned about changing its existences on the earth plane. Spirit does not mind whether the body it inhabits is black-skinned or white-skinned; tall or short; female or male. It is the Spirit's overall destiny that is important, not the type of body it abides in. As you already know, the Spirit can vacate one body and be newly born into another one, thousands of miles away, within minutes. So you see, the Spirit lives on. Fulfilling its destiny is what counts.'

I still could not understand why the Spirit would want to kill off a current physical existence in order to begin another one. It did not make sense. Reading my thoughts, the Guide explained.

'It makes sense if you want to achieve something,' he said sternly. 'Let me put it this way. Supposing you develop a lesion on the brain. This lesion affects your body's balance, and, consequently, you acquire a stagger. The stagger pulls you to the right all the time; you cannot walk in a straight line, no matter how hard you try. You reach a point where you have no food in the house. You need food but you can never reach the market because you keep going around in circles. Each time you leave your front door you veer to the right; you keep on veering right all around the perimeter of the house, until you arrive back at your front door again. This way, you never manage to get any food. Each day you try, and each day you fail. You are slowly dying of hunger. And you know you are dying of hunger. There is nothing you can do about it. The body you so badly depend on has developed a fault, one that cannot be corrected. So what do you do? Do you keep on going around in circles until you drop?

'This is the situation with the Spirit whose Ego fails to respond to the Spirit's wishes. Rather than spend its precious time going around in circles, the Spirit withdraws; it starts again and, hopefully, in more facilitating conditions.'

Now I had a clearer picture of destiny and the Spirit's purpose in the scheme of things. But I had two more questions before my picture was complete.

'What about all the people who die young?' I asked. 'Does this mean that these people would not have fulfilled their respective destinies if they had lived a long life?'

'No. Not necessarily,' the Guide answered. 'Many of those who die young have already achieved their purpose in life. Bear in mind that fulfilling a destiny does not always demand the doing of great deeds. An individual's deceased parent could incarnate into the body of the individual's grandchild, just to bring a few years of joy to that individual. Once that task had been achieved, then there would be no necessity for the Spirit to continue its life on earth.'

I wondered about babies who die at birth or shortly afterwards. Did they, too, fulfil some sort of purpose?

In reply to this question, the Guide answered. 'Again, this is the work of the Spirit. Sometimes, in its eagerness to incarnate, the Spirit may end up in circumstances that do not have the necessary potential to fulfil its destiny. Once the Spirit becomes aware of this, all it can do is withdraw.'

Reincarnation

So far, I learned from the Guides that incarnation and reincarnation are necessary and inevitable in the perpetual process of evolution. The Soul/Spirit accumulates knowledge in each incarnation by carrying out various tasks and functions. The tasks, functions and consequent experiences of each lifetime are commensurate with the Spirit's destiny, its blueprint for evolution, and its overall bias to balance.

All very well, but why so much suffering in this world? Why could not the Soul/Spirit exist on earth, learn what it has to learn, and not have to suffer?

The Guide explained, 'On one hand, suffering is central to the process of learning; on the other hand, it is not. Suffering comes from three sources: the Ego-mind, the Spirit, and the Law of Karma. The suffering of the Ego-mind is unnecessary suffering; the suffering of the Spirit, optional; and the Law of Karma, essential.

'The Ego-mind is a creature of extremes. It goes to great extremes to satisfy its voracious appetite for wealth, sensory satisfaction and egoistic power. And, in its excessive quest for these things, it not only creates its own suffering, but also often causes suffering to others. Individuals bring suffering on themselves all the time through overwork, eating too much of the wrong foods, drinking too much alcohol, taking drugs, smoking cigarettes, insufficient physical exercise and so on. All these things result in suffering. They are caused by the folly of the Ego-mind. This type of suffering is unnecessary; it can be eradicated by introducing positive, balanced actions into daily life.

'Suffering can also be created by the Spirit. Generally, when the Spirit introduces suffering into an individual's life, it is done in order to force the individual to learn a particular lesson. If the individual learns this lesson, and changes his life accordingly, the suffering will cease. Also, the Spirit will sometimes incarnate into a life of suffering in order to learn from the experience of suffering. This type of suffering is chosen by the Spirit in order to evolve consciousness.

'The third type of suffering is governed by the Law of Karma, and is unavoidable. The Law of Karma is the Cosmic law of cause and effect: for every action, there is an equal and opposite reaction. This law carries the inherent Cosmic intent towards balance; this same intent towards balance is echoed in the Spirit.

'Bear in mind that existence is an ongoing process. The actions of past lives can come to fruition, for better or worse, in a future life. It may well be that the hunter will become the hunted; the slave-master, the slave; the perpetrator, the victim; and the abuser, the abused.'

I thought about what the Guide said, but still did not fully understand how the Law of Karma worked in relation to sequential existences. How did cause and effect balance out? I queried this.

The Guide stayed silent for a number of seconds before replying. 'Let us take the slave-master and the slave for our example. In the present lifetime, the slave-master uses the slave for twenty years. Then the roles are reversed and in the next lifetime the slave-master is the slave, and he is used for twenty years by the slave, who is now the slave-master. In this way the Karmic slate is wiped clean on both sides: both parties have served twenty years in opposite conditions, and so, a balance is brought about. From that point onwards, if the two Souls/Spirits in our example devote their time to self-development and self-realisation, then their positive actions will produce positive effects in their future lives. This example serves as a rough sketch only. Each individual's case is different. Each case will comprise different degrees and variations of this or that, according to how each individual's life has been lived. But the basic rule of thumb is: those who promote scarcity and hunger will return in another life to suffer scarcity and hunger; those who pollute will become the victims of pollution; and so on.'

'Is God in any way instrumental in executing the Law of Karma?' I asked.

'God is instrumental in everything, but it is, ultimately, the individual's own Spirit that acts as judge and jury of its own being. When the physical body is cast off [dies], and before the Soul passes into the astral realms, the Spirit replays and examines the Soul-memory of its recent life on earth. From watching the replay, the Spirit sees the imbalances in the totality of its being. For example, during the recent life, because of a certain characteristic or character flaw, the individual may have caused pain to others. If that flaw was not corrected in the recent lifetime, it will have to be dealt with in the next. Likewise, in order for the Karmic debt to be paid, the pain inflicted on others will also have to be suffered by the individual in the next lifetime. In this way, the individual will receive what he or she has given.'

'What about those who inflict pain and misery on millions of people? How will the Law of Karma affect these people?' I inquired.

'Their own respective Spirits will take care of these matters,' the Guide replied curtly. 'The point of this lesson is to emphasise the need for balance in every individual's life. If suffering on earth were diminished by the actions of a particular generation of souls, then the need for suffering would diminish during that generation's next incarnation.

'Let us take two groups of individuals, for example. There are one thousand individuals in each group. The first is group "A"; the second, group "B." Group A are wealthy, powerful people; they control and manipulate much of the world's wealth. Let us say that these people, through interference and manipulation, have drained a small country of its resources. This country is almost on its knees when a drought comes along. There are no crops and no food; millions of people suffer the agony of starvation and slow death. But this does not concern group A. They are too involved in accumulating wealth.

'Along comes group B. These are aid workers. They place themselves at the disposal of the famine victims and help in every way that they can. They want nothing for themselves; they simply want to help.'

'The one thousand people of group A die and are reborn. But now there is a Karmic debt to be paid. And so, group A are reborn into an area that will be hit by famine. Therefore, they will suffer in the same way that they themselves have caused suffering. But here is the crux of the matter: if group A had not caused the suffering in the first instance, there would be no need for them to suffer in the second.'

'On the other hand, group B acted in accordance with the way of the Spirit; they helped other human beings. By doing so they have raised themselves to a higher evolutionary level and will be re-born into balanced conditions. That is how the Law of Karma works. If individuals sow the seeds of peace, harmony, justice and altruism in this life, then they will reap the benefits of their actions in succeeding lives.'

'Furthermore, if each and every individual on earth created a balance within themselves, a balance of circumstances would result throughout the entire planet. Let us say, for example, that human greed is taken out of the picture. In this case, the resources of the planet would be shared equally among all individuals; you would not find circumstances of extreme wealth in one place and extreme poverty in another. And because they have created an equable environment on earth in this lifetime, they will have an equable environment to be born into in their future lives. As you can see, balance is the antidote to human suffering, both on an individual and a collective level.'

'How long does the Soul/Spirit spend in the spirit world before it reincarnates?' I asked.

'There is no set time,' the Guide said. 'It can be a few minutes or a few thousand years. Bear in mind that time, as you know it, is an illusion. Another illusion is the fact that people, in general, tend to speak of "future generations." But who are the future generations? They are the Souls/Spirits of today – *you*. The future generations of your world are you, your family, friends, and the majority of people that exist in the world today.

'Consider carefully what I have just said. It should be of particular interest to those who create and promote narcotic drugs, alcohol, tobacco, toxic chemicals and other pollutants. There is an inescapable, ironic justice inherent in the Law of Karma: those who peddle destruction will suffer accordingly in future lifetimes.'

Shortly after going to sleep that night, I had a dream. In the dream I had physically died and had entered a world of silver-white vapour. I was quite conscious of all that had taken place; I knew that I had passed over into the spirit realm. I also knew that I had to return to earth to be born again into another physical body. There were no emotional feelings about this, it was simply an observation. Next, I felt a pull, as if I were being drawn by a giant magnet, and I knew, at that moment, that I was being pulled into a new birth. I could not believe how quickly it had all happened. In the dream, the time-period between this life and the next amounted to no more than a few minutes.

The next morning, another question came to mind. If we lived so many lives on earth in different circumstances, why can we not remember all of these past lives?

When I put this question to the Guide, he told me, 'But you can remember your past lives. And you know this. Past-life memories lie barely below the level of everyday consciousness. They can be accessed by hypnosis [past-life regression], and as you know, they can sometimes surface in dreams. It is also known that precocious talents, phobias and aversions have their origins in past lives. So, Soul-memories are not as deeply buried as you might think.'

'But why can we not just sit down in an armchair and remember our past lives, as we would when recalling nostalgic memories from this life?' I asked.

'Because you are meant to focus on this life. The reality of your entire, eternal existence is in this moment. When you are born into this life, a "new" Ego-consciousness is born; a consciousness that gives the individual an opportunity to evolve and progress without the influence of past-life memories. But if you particularly want to evoke past-life memories, you can. All you have to do is relax in meditation, or before sleep, and cast your mind back to the time of your birth and before your birth. In meditation you will receive images and impressions from a past life; in sleep you will dream of the past life. Your success will depend on the power of your *intent*, your *will* to evoke past-life memories.

'One more question,' I said. 'Is it possible for the Soul/Spirit, after living life in human form, to reincarnate into animal form?'

'It is not uncommon,' said the Guide. 'Sometimes the Soul/Spirit may choose a life in animal form in order to learn a particular lesson.'

Life after Death

The following discussion arose out of a question regarding the silver–white thread which the Guide had mentioned in talking about the structure of the Cosmos and the 'Nature Of God'. I asked for more information about this energy thread. The Guide went on to explain.

'The silver thread is a thin cord of energy that links each unit of energy/consciousness to the Central Sphere, the Source. It acts not only as a link, but also as a conduit for "impulses" of pure energy from the Source to the individual. It is also a conduit for the return of consciousness to the higher planes.

'This energy thread is connected to the etheric body of each being; and as you know, the etheric body is a dense sheath of energy that surrounds, works through, and maintains the well-being of the physical body. Without the energy of the etheric body, the energy of the physical body would be dangerously low [which may explain why the physical body experiences temporary paralysis when the etheric body is projected]. Bear in mind that the silver thread does not carry vital energy, but energy impulses. The etheric body uses the chakras – especially the Solar Plexus chakra – to draw the required amount of vital energy from the ether.

'At the moment of death, when the heart stops beating, the energy of the physical body withdraws from the four physical elements – earth, air, fire and water. At this point the energy enters the etheric field. Generally, when this stage is reached, the silver thread disconnects from the etheric body and retracts into the subtle energy of the astral planes bringing with it the individual's consciousness. This consciousness now consists of the astral, emotional, mental, psychic and spiritual energy fields. As the silver thread, with consciousness attached, "recoils" into the realms of refined energy, it gives rise to an experience of travelling at high speed through a tunnel. You have read reported cases of near-death experiences, and as you know, the end of the tunnel gives way to a brilliant, bright light. This is the Light of Spirit, or the Realm of Spirit.

'In the Realm of Spirit there are many worlds, and it is in one of these worlds that the Soul/Spirit will rest while it decides what action is necessary for further evolution [learning]. Sometimes, because of a strong mental or emotional attachment to the earth plane, or because of a desire to repay a Karmic debt, the Soul/Spirit will reincarnate directly, without resting in the higher worlds. Where the Soul/Spirit rests will depend on the energy frequency of the individual. As we have said before, Cosmic energy frequencies range from very fine in the God-Realm, to the very dense in the world of matter. But in cases of physical death, the four elements of matter and the denser frequency of ether are redundant; therefore, the lowest frequencies an individual can experience in the after-death state are the lower astral worlds and the astral sub-planes. If individuals wish to return to the world of matter, then they will do so by way of being reborn in a physical body on the earth plane.

'There is another state in which the Soul/Spirit can exist: one that makes use of the etheric body. The state I refer to is what you know as an "earth-bound" state. It happens when the Soul/Spirit becomes trapped between the worlds of spirit and the world of matter.'

This was a subject that had intrigued me for many years. "Earthbound" spirits are what we commonly call "ghosts," and, having grown up in rural Ireland during the fifties and sixties, I was no stranger to the concept of non-material beings. Having said that, I have never seen a ghost "in the flesh," so to speak. By this I mean that I have never, with my sense of physical sight, seen a spirit in human, corporeal form. It was this thought that ran through my mind when the Guide mentioned "earthbound" spirits.

'But you have seen an earthbound Spirit,' the Guide said. 'Though not with your physical eyes. Think back to the tramp you met...'

The familiar image of a tramp came to mind. I had met this particular tramp while "out-of-body" one day (14 May 1995). I was walking along an empty street in my "out-of-body" state, when, out of nowhere, the tramp ran over to me and began talking effusively. It was as if he had not spoken to anyone in a long time; hence his eagerness to communicate. At the time, I had no idea of who, or what, the tramp was.

'. . . He is and earthbound individual,' continued the Guide.

'Why is he earthbound?' I asked.

'Because he does not realise that he has separated from his physical body. He thinks he is still made of flesh and bone, so he carries on living as he has always lived. He walks the streets begging for money, but no one sees or hears him. This is not incongruous as far as the tramp's consciousness is concerned. When he inhabited his physical body and begged on the streets, people pretended not to see or hear him. So, to him, there is not much difference between then and now.

I became intrigued by this conversation and wanted to know more about the tramp's situation.

'Does he get hungry?' I asked.

'When he sees food, he feels hunger. But it is not real hunger. It is simply a feeling; an habitual reaction to food. He also feels the need for alcohol, just as he did when in the physical body.'

I thought of how tantalizing it must be for the tramp. In his invisible state he could invite himself into the top restaurants in town, see the tables laden with sumptuous food and vintage wine, and not be able to sample a drop of wine or a morsel of food.

'It is not like that,' commented the Guide, reading my thoughts. 'The tramp was never allowed to enter those premises during his physical existence, and, because he still considers himself "alive," he will not venture where he is not wanted. He haunts the back alleys and parks, as always. And he does manage to satisfy his need for alcohol.'

This statement surprised me more than any so far.

'Yes,' he continued, 'he can "consume" alcohol by inhaling the fumes. When disembodied entities "suck" alcohol from an open can or bottle, they think they are imbibing liquid, but it is the etheric fumes of the alcohol that they experience.'

'Do they get drunk?' I asked.

'No, not drunk in the real sense of the word. They convince themselves of the effects of the alcohol, but in reality, the jubilation they feel is a state of mind – it is psychological.'

'So,' I said, 'if the tramp wanted, he could go into any pub and make himself feel good by inhaling or "imbibing" alcohol fumes from peoples' drinking glasses.'

'But he does not,' the Guide responded. 'He had not patronised public houses for many years before his physical death, and he does not do so now. Such is the power of mental conditioning: it carries through from one existence to the next. As I have said, the tramp occupies the parks and alleyways seeking like-minded individuals to get involved with and to influence.'

I was on the point of asking what he meant by "like-minded individuals to get involved with and to influence," but the Guide anticipated my question and went on to explain.

'The tramp will seek the company of what you call "winos" and groups of individuals who sit in parks drinking beer, wine and cider. He will involve himself in their parties.'

'But how can he manage that if he cannot communicate with those who are alive?'

'He can hear what they say and listen to their banter and repartee. But he cannot hear in the same way as if he had sensory hearing. His energy body receives the voice vibrations of the speakers. The voices that he hears sound distant. He interprets this as partial deafness, and because no one hears him when he speaks, he thinks that everyone else is completely deaf.'

'You mentioned something about the tramp "seeking to influence." Tell me more about that,' I said.

'Yes. At times when alcohol is not available and when drinking groups are not to be found, the tramp will seek out drinkers that are known to him and "suggest" that they start drinking and begin a party. This suggestion is directed telepathically at the "living" drinker, who receives the thought as an impulse – an urge to start drinking. Once the drinker responds to the impulse and starts a drinking bout, the alcohol opens his psyche, leaving him more and more susceptible to the tramp's suggestions.'

'Does this mean that the tramp's spirit possesses the drinker?' I asked.

The Guide thought for a moment. 'No, not possesses – strongly influences. The tramp can take control while the drinker is physically weakened from the after-effects of the previous day's alcohol, or while the drinker is intoxicated. When the drinker reaches a highly intoxicated state, the tramp may vent his frustration, and sometimes his anger and violence, through the drinker, causing the drinker to lash out at whoever is close by. While the tramp is in control, the drinker's features will change and he will be seen to undergo a personality change. Consequently, when he becomes sober he will have no recollection of his angry or violent actions while he was intoxicated.'

To me this sounded very much like spirit possession.

'Perhaps it could be viewed as partial possession,' suggested the Guide. 'But the drinker regains control of his own life, providing he stops taking alcohol. Once the drinker initiates an intent to stop drinking, and carries out that intent, then the tramp will leave him alone and go off in search of someone else to influence.'

'Does this mean that the majority of alcohol drinkers are being adversely influenced by the earthbound spirits of "dead" drinkers?' I asked.

'No,' replied the Guide. 'Not all. But it is common. When an individual experiences repeated compulsions to drink alcohol, then he may be influenced by an external entity. When these compulsions are experienced, the individual is driven towards alcohol, as if in a dream. He wonders why he is on his way to drink alcohol, but he cannot find any logical reason for doing so. Yet he is pushed along by an invisible force. Even when the individual takes the first sip from his drink, he will still be puzzled as to why he is doing it.'

'If a person experiences this "symptom," what should he or she do?' I inquired.

'Go to a spiritual healer immediately,' the Guide emphasised.

Thinking about "compulsions" and a subsequent loss of control, I wondered if a person could be influenced in the same way when gambling.

'Yes," the Guide said, 'in cases where the "gambler" is no longer in control: where he sets out to bet on the winner of a race and ends up betting on a loser; or where he intends to bet a certain amount of money but may be "coerced" into betting substantially more.'

I got the feeling that earthbound spirits were more numerous than I had ever imagined.

'Almost all places of gambling and drinking have their own particular "ghosts,"' said the Guide. 'But it is only those who are the most psychic who fall prey to the entity's influence.'

'Why are all these souls earthbound?' I asked.

'To explain that, let us get back to the tramp. Firstly, the tramp does not know he is dead; therefore, he does not seek the higher realms. Secondly, he is ignorant of spiritual matters, and the reality of the Spirit worlds are unknown to him. Thirdly, the tramp is fettered to the material world by the material lusts of his Ego-mind. It is mainly his desire for alcohol that keeps him in his gross etheric state. If the tramp were a man of prayer and spiritual ideals, even if he did not know of his physical demise, he would eventually gravitate towards the Light and enter the world of Spirit.'

'Will the tramp be earthbound for all eternity?' I inquired.

'Not necessarily. As it stands, the tramp has no family to pray for him and no one to guide him across; therefore, he is helpless from a spiritual point of view. But there are ways that he can be helped. Someone, like yourself, could meet him on the etheric plane and urge him to let go of his etheric body. You could tell him of his death and how to pray. You could pray with him, and for him, and "will" him towards the Light. Or you could invoke the assistance of an angelic being to help the tramp across. But perhaps the quickest and most assured way of ascending to the higher planes is for the tramp to have a fatal accident.'

This astonished me. I asked how the "dead" tramp could manage to have a "fatal" accident.

'He could be killed by a car,' the Guide said.

As I tried to figure out how that could be achieved, I noticed a flicker of amusement in the Guide's eyes. After a few seconds of silence, he began to explain.

'If he were crossing a busy road and got struck by a speeding car, he would be killed. That is how the tramp would perceive it.'

I interrupted to ask if the car, that he spoke of, was a "real" car or a car of astral substance.

'A real car,' he said. 'Bear in mind that the etheric body is close in density to the physical body; thus, the shock of being hit by a speeding solid object would snap the silver thread and yank the tramp's consciousness from the etheric body. At that point, the tramp would see the Light of Spirit. If he accepted this condition, he would rest in the Spirit Realm; but if his desire for the earth plane is still strong, then he will immediately incarnate into another physical body.'

I wondered what would happen to the tramp's etheric body once his consciousness had withdrawn from it. I had read once that the etheric body gradually disintegrates. It was suggested by the author of that book that etheric bodies in the process of disintegration could account for many of the hideous, ghoulish forms (sometimes referred to as "shades") that are depicted in connection with graveyards.

In answer to my thoughts, the Guide said, 'That is true. The form of the etheric body does disintegrate, but not the energy – the form only. After a period of time, the etheric energy itself returns to its formless state.

'When the physical body is dead and when the astral, emotional, mental, psychic and spiritual bodies have withdrawn, then the etheric form is left "empty." For a number of days after the physical death of the individual, the etheric form may wander around, seemingly in a somnambulistic state. At this point it will not possess consciousness, *per se*, but it will be attracted to familiar energy emanations from the individual's house and possessions. In some cases, the etheric body may still be linked to the corpse and may accompany it to its graveyard resting place. But as you have read, this connection does pass away – usually after twenty-one days – and the etheric energy then returns to the ether.'

'Can earthbound souls reincarnate?' I asked.

'No. Consciousness must first return to the subtle planes, and then the non-attached entity can incarnate once again.'

'What causes a Spirit to be earthbound?' I inquired.

'Quite often individuals do not realise they are dead, especially in cases of sudden death where the gradual process of withdrawing has not been experienced. The individual wakes up from unconsciousness, or from a death sleep, and his Ego-mind, as usual, finds itself in the physical world.'

This reminded me of an experience I had had with a friend of mine who passed away. For a time after his death, a small, electric-blue light kept appearing in our apartment. The light was a vertical strip about one inch in width and about two-and-a-half to three inches in height. On a daily and nightly basis it appeared to my clairvoyant sight, floating about four to five feet off the ground, in various rooms of the apartment. Coinciding with the blue light was an even stranger phenomenon: if the blue light appeared in a room while the electric light was on, the light bulb in that room would crackle and make popping sounds, like a light bulb "blowing." I sensed that the blue light was the spirit of my friend, but I thought that he would leave the earth plane in his own good time, so I ignored the phenomenon.

Three weeks passed and the blue light kept on appearing, accompanied at night time by the unusual crackling and popping noises from the light bulbs. One night, shortly after twelve o'clock, as I lay on my back in bed, the blue light appeared at the foot of the bed and hovered at a height of around five feet. In the darkness of the bedroom, the light looked brighter than ever before. At that moment in time, I knew that I would have to give in and communicate with my friend. As I mentioned in 'Book I', I have a propensity to mediumship, but it is a talent that I am reluctant to exercise. However, there are times when fears and concerns have to be put aside.

I closed my eyes, relaxed, and pictured myself standing in the bedroom, outside my physical body. In an instant, my friend stood before me. He looked just as he did when he was "alive." He grinned and greeted me, delighted with our contact, and although I "replied" to him telepathically, he did not notice anything unusual about this. He said that he had wondered what had "gone wrong" with everyone as no one would speak to him or acknowledge his presence. He wondered if it were all part of a crazy dream. He reported that he had been dreaming a lot of late, and that some of those vivid dreams were quite unnerving. In one dream he was viewing his own coffin in the funeral parlour; in another he saw a group of people on their way to his funeral. He asked me if he had gone mad or had everyone else lost their sanity. As much as I did not want to deliver the news that he was dead, I had to – there was no other option. When I told him, his first reaction was that of disbelief; he accused me of trying to play a sick joke on him. In an effort to convince him, I discussed certain details of the incidents he had witnessed during the three-week period and brought his attention to certain "proofs" contained therein.

When he finally accepted the fact that he was dead, emotional devastation followed. I have never seen a person weep so uncontrollably! At this juncture his concern was not for himself, but for his family. When he finally calmed down, my next task was to convince him of the futility of hanging on to the earth plane. I told him that he must let go and allow himself to enter the higher worlds.

Fortunately, about a month or two before this incident, I had read *The Tibetan Book of Living and Dying*, in which the author, Sogyal Rinpoche, tells us how to use The Essential Phowa Practice to help the dying, and in this case, the recently dead. Firstly, my friend and I "went" outside the building. On my instructions we stood and looked towards the south. I urged my friend to visualise a bright orb of light, like a brilliant sun in the night sky, close to the horizon. I joined him in this visualisation practice to strengthen the "intent" of the procedure. Because this man had a Christian background, I visualised the images of Christ and the Virgin Mary at either side of the orb of light. Time and time again, I asked my friend if he could "see" the light, but he replied "no" every time. This compelled me to visualise more forcefully.

Eventually, in response to my questioning, he said that he could now see the light; it was coming towards him. 'It's getting bigger,' he said. 'It's nearly here.' Then he said something that really shocked me: 'Oh, look! There's my father.' Obviously, my friend's "deceased" father had come to help him into the Realm of Spirit. I exhorted my friend to let go of this world and to go along with his father. To that there was no reply. When I looked towards where he had stood, I realised why. His Spirit was not there any more. He had gone into the Realm of Light.

When I returned to everyday consciousness, my physical body was bathed in perspiration. It was as if a basin of water had been thrown on me. Both my mouth and throat were uncomfortably dry. Getting up to get a drink of water, I saw that the time was 2.35 a.m.. Two-and-a-half hours had passed, in a time-span that had seemed like twenty minutes.

In a discussion on the subject of 'Destiny,' the Guide said that when an individual lives life contrary to his destiny, the Spirit often engineers physical illness and accidents in order to give the individual a shock – to wake him up. Quite often, too, the Spirit causes physical death when it sees that its plans (destiny) might be thwarted. If the Spirit is so powerful in these cases, I wondered why does it not have the power to lead the individual to his rightful place after death.

'It does have the power,' the Guide answered. 'It has the power to reincarnate when it needs to do so. It knows its own energy frequency and to what "heights" it can go in the astral worlds. It knows the lessons it needs in order to bring it to a higher arc of evolution. It knows all these things, and it has the power to accomplish these things, but sadly for the Spirit, the Ego-mind gets in the way.

'Bear in mind that Ego-consciousness does not die with the physical body. All that the Ego contains – attachment to worldly things, desire, penchant for pleasure, preconceptions, philosophical concepts, beliefs, hatreds, hopes and fears – all these things are carried over into the after-life. This baggage can be cumbersome for the Spirit to deal with.'

I thought of what the Guide had once told me about the Soul/Spirit staying in the astral worlds for perhaps a thousand years, or more, before considering reincarnating. I asked if the Ego-mind with all its foibles remained intact throughout this period.

'Yes,' the Guide said. 'That is so. The Ego-mind does not necessarily change its attitude or characteristics in the astral realms. However, those who hanker for material things and a material existence will not stay in the astral realms for a thousand years; they will reincarnate very quickly. And each time the Soul/Spirit reincarnates, the contents of the existing Ego-mind are absorbed into the Soul. In other words, the existing Ego effectively dies prior to each "new" physical birth.

'But as we have said, the existing Ego-mind does hinder the Spirit's progress, both in this life and the next. Therefore, if you want to make things easier in this life and in the next, it is advisable to dissolve the power of the Ego.

The Ego

Many times, in the course of the teachings, the Guides had exhorted me to "dissolve the power of the Ego," or as they sometimes put it, "transcend the Ego." I was still unclear about the meaning of this particular counsel. From my limited reading on the subject of psychology, I understood that the Ego was the "I," the sense of "self" in all of us. This being the case, how was I to dissolve my own sense of self?

When I asked this question, the Guides told me that when they spoke of the "Ego," they meant Ego-consciousness or the Ego-mind. They went on to say that I, like most of my fellow human beings, perceived the world from a level of consciousness that was Ego-based. Consciousness that is Ego-based, they said, is flawed; therefore, it presented illusory perceptions of self and the world in general. For this reason, consciousness must be wrenched from the grasp of the Ego. and be raised to the abode of the True Self, the realm of Reality.

Harking back to psychology, I had learned that there are three aspects to everyday consciousness: the Id, the Ego, and the Super-ego. Some branches of psychoanalysis refer to these three components as the "Child," the "Adult," and the "Parent," respectively. The Id/Child provides us with our ideas, desires, whims, hopes and dreams. The Super-ego/Parent vets our ideas and whims, and curtails inclinations towards distasteful behaviour; in other words, it is what we call "conscience." These two components can be seen at work in our daily lives. For example, when the Id/Child aspect is ascendant we may say, or do, something daft on the spur of the moment. Afterwards, on reflection, the Super-ego/Parent may castigate us for our foolishness; thus we end up feeling embarrassed by, and regretting, our impropriety. The third aspect of everyday consciousness is the Adult/Ego. This aspect encourages us to take responsibility for ourselves, our communities and our environment. It maintains our sense of reality, without the capriciousness of the Id/Child and the severity of the Super-ego/Parent. The Adult/Ego encourages us to be "real," calculating and down to earth.

I wondered how these three aspects of consciousness related to the "Ego-mind" that the Guides advised me to "dissolve" or "transcend."

The Guide explained: 'When we speak of "Ego-mind," "Ego-conscious-ness," or "Ego-self" we are talking about a *level* of consciousness, and not an *aspect* of consciousness. We are talking about Ego-consciousness as a *whole*. For convenience, we will refer to the totality of the Ego-consciousness as the "Ego," and you can bear in mind that this term encompasses all three aspects of consciousness as you have outlined them [the Id, Ego and Super-ego].

'The Ego, as a whole, is a "new" consciousness. It begins at birth and develops parallel to physical growth. By the time the growth of the physical body has reached maturity, the Ego is firmly established and in full control of the individual. Now the Ego has developed a solid sense of "self" and a firm perception of its relationship with the world. The Ego may perceive itself to be strong, clever, sophisticated, all-knowing, beautiful, glamorous, wise or any combination of adjectives that will reinforce, and enhance, its sense of individuality, its sense of self [i.e., "I am a very clever, sophisticated person"]. Regarding its relationship with the world, the Ego usually identifies its "self" with its material possessions, its occupation, its social status and its religious belief ["I am a botanist", "I am the chair-person of the local tennis club", or "I am a Christian"]. Consider this: Are any of the self-enhancing adjectives the real individual? Are material possessions the real individual? Is the individual's occupation, social standing or religious belief the real individual?'

I thought about the Guide's questions for a moment or two, and it became evident that the answer was an emphatic "no" to all three questions. How people thought of themselves, what people owned, what people believed in, and the activities that they became involved in, clearly were not the eternal individuals themselves.

The Guide asked, 'And why does the Ego identify itself with external things? Why does it develop this false sense of self? Because it has learned to do so. Remember that at birth the Ego is "new." It is devoid of opinions and beliefs until it learns from its parents, older siblings, relatives, friends, teachers, employers, reading material, radio and television. All that the Ego sees and hears comes from the external world; therefore, the Ego becomes increasingly dependent on feedback from the external world for its sense of reality and its sense of "self." But, as the Ego continues to absorb external stimuli, it gradually becomes a conglomeration of other individuals' opinions, notions, beliefs, emotional reactions and behavioural patterns.

'Certain learned behaviour patterns can be detrimental. An Ego may learn that scheming, stealing, deceiving, throwing temper tantrums or being aggressive is the only way to get what it wants. And as you know, these ways of thinking, feeling and acting are unnecessary. Each and every individual can achieve, and acquire, what they want by nurturing their own creative talents and skills and by using their energy and creativity, in the service of others. But, until the Ego learns this, it will carry on thinking, feeling and acting destructively, if this is how it has learned to behave.

'And when particular thinking patterns become frozen in the Ego-mind, consciousness becomes limited, self-centered and inflexible. At this point, it separates, and puts itself above those who do not share the same opinions and beliefs. It functions under the illusion that its opinions, its outlook on life, and its political and religious beliefs are sacrosanct; therefore, all incompatible opinions and beliefs are wrong. Not only that, but it also condemns all individuals who harbour incompatible opinions and beliefs, and may label those same individuals as "bad." More often than not, this type of rigid thinking leads to personal conflicts [war within the self], breakdowns in relationships, rifts in communities – and ultimately, wars.

'To say all there is to say about the human Ego-mind would take a long, long time. Most of what we have to say would be unflattering, if not insulting, to some. The Ego is a sensitive creature. It is easily wounded, especially when its self-image is threatened or challenged. Suffice it to say that the brief overview I have given you demonstrates how delusive and destructive the Ego can be. Not only that, but the Ego also continuously creates and maintains an illusory existence for itself. In order to escape this world of illusion, consciousness must be raised to the abode of the True Self, the realm of Reality.'

The True Self

'What exactly is the "True Self," and what is the difference between the True Self and the Ego-self,' I asked.

'The True Self is the Spiritual Self, the Real Self, the Timeless Self, the Eternal Self, the Infinite Self. In the Realm of the True Self everything just is. And the way of the True Self is to *be* – *to be itself*. Conversely, the Ego-self is the limited self; the self who thinks it is something other than what it actually is. While the True Self is expansive and eternal, the Ego-self is finite and impermanent. It is impermanent because it can be eliminated from existence.

''But you told me that the Ego-self does not die,' I pointed out. 'You said that the Ego-mind of this life carries over to the next.'

'That is true,' answered the Guide. 'Perhaps we did not make ourselves clear. When we talked about "Ego-mind" we were talking about a level of consciousness; now we are talking about the Ego-self, the contents of the Ego that constitute the Ego's self-image. By "contents" we mean the illusory mental and emotional baggage that the Ego-mind accumulates during the course of its earthly existence. It is necessary to rid yourself of this baggage if you want to become acquainted with your True Self.

'But you cannot know the True Self in the same way as the Ego-self. You can put the Ego-self under a microscope and examine all its various components – characteristics, attributes, habits and the like. But you cannot examine the True Self in this way. The True Self is not a thing; it is not an item to be studied. The True Self can only be experienced.

'An expression of the True Self is what you would call a "state of spirituality." And those whose consciousness dwells in the Realm of the True Self are usually defined as "spiritual." Do not confuse spirituality with religion. A religious individual is one who rigidly adheres to established concepts, beliefs, dogma and ritualistic practices. Spirituality is *not* a concept, theory, dogma or ritual. It is, first and foremost, a *state of being*. It is a way of life. It is a practice. Those who are truly spiritual dedicate their lives to the service of God's creatures – the sick, the poor, the perturbed, the dying and the homeless, human and animal alike. In other words, the sole aspiration of a spiritual individual is to relieve pain and suffering, and to contribute to the general welfare of the planet, and all thereon. But before we move on from our reference to religion, there is something you must bear in mind. Not many spiritual individuals are religious; and not many religious individuals are spiritual. A spiritual person can be easily identified by their understanding, compassion, love, a sense of peace and harmony, and by the way they respect and work in the interest of all living things. But these characteristics are not spirituality itself; they are manifestations, or expressions, of spirituality that work through an individual whose consciousness has become harmonised and *whole*.

'The experience of spirituality cannot be described with words. We could talk about inner peace, harmony and bliss, but until you experience this state for yourself, the words we use are meaningless to you. Listen to the following story, and contemplate the difference between the Ego-self and the True Self.

'This story is about the Seeker: an individual who sets out to find a magic Shrine. The Seeker has, on many occasions, listened to accounts of the Shrine and its extraordinary powers. From the stories he has heard, the Seeker knows that the Shrine is a sacred place of healing, unity and wholeness; a place of harmony, happiness and true freedom. It is a place of the gods. But the Seeker does not know where the Shrine is located. From what he has learned from other seekers, the Shrine is situated on a high hill. The forested hillside and surrounding valley make it impossible for the Shrine to be seen from below.

'The Seeker sets out on his journey. He has heard that there are many paths to the Shrine; some are dead-ends, but most lead all the way to the hill's summit. Eventually, the Seeker finds a path. He does not know if it is the right path, but the only way to find out is to travel it. Soon he comes to a signpost. The signpost has a metal plate bolted on to it; this plate is pointed at one end and turned in the direction the Seeker is travelling. Written on the metal plate is the word, "Shrine."

'The Seeker is delighted with this discovery, but he is ignorant of what the Shrine really is, or what it is supposed to be like. Soon, a dilemma develops. Does the pointed sign mean that the Shrine is further on, or does the word, "Shrine," written on the metal plate mean that the sign, itself, is the Shrine? And so, the Seeker sits down before the signpost and contemplates the word, "Shrine." He becomes immersed in his contemplation. He convinces himself that he feels the harmony, happiness and joy synonymous with the stories he had heard of the true Shrine. So there the Seeker sits, day after day, looking at the word, "Shrine," trying to divine the word's spiritual message, and trying, with all his heart, to feel what spirituality might be like.

'Weeks pass. The Seeker cannot tear himself away from the sign. A voice within tells him that he is not at the true Shrine, but it is too late; the Seeker already believes that he is at the true Shrine.

'One day, a group of seekers comes along. The Seeker is overjoyed to have company and to have someone to share his great discovery. He introduces the seekers to the sign and tells them that it is the Shrine. They, too, sit down and contemplate the sign. Over and over, they read the word "Shrine," and day after day, they try to interpret its "spiritual" meaning.

'Days pass, and other groups of seekers come along; they, too, are introduced to the sign. They, too, are encouraged to read the word "Shrine," over and over, in order to decipher its meaning. And, hour after hour, debates arise. One group believes that the word, "Shrine," is the true Shrine; another believes that the metal plate that supports the word is the true Shrine. Another group believes that the sign's post is the Shrine; others are adamant that the true shrine is the nuts and bolts that clamp the metal plate to the signpost. Time and time again, squabbles break out, and hostility and hatred grow between the groups of different beliefs and opinions. And as other groups of seekers come along, they, too, are dragged into the fray. All newcomers are forced to believe one thing or another; they are forced to surrender their loyalties to one group or another. Those who refuse to do so are persecuted. And so it goes on, year in and year out, one group against another. Ironically, the groups become so busy fighting and defending their respective beliefs, that they forget all about their search for the true Shrine. They even forget about the sign, "Shrine," that they fight over.

'Disgusted by the behaviour of his peers, the Seeker, in the hours of darkness, escapes from the established camps. Having no alternative, he travels the path in the direction he was travelling at the outset of his search. Before dawn, the Seeker comes upon the true Shrine. When the Seeker arrives at the summit of the hill, he sees that the Shrine is a block of stone. But this is no ordinary stone – it has the power to transform all those who enter its presence. It is also wise and ageless, having neither a beginning, nor an end. Its form manifested from the formless, and its form will one day return to the formless. But even in its formless state, the Shrine will never cease to be a Shrine.

'The Seeker climbs on top of the stone block and looks down the forested hillside. In the light of dawn, he sees that there are many paths that lead to the Shrine. He notices that one is not different from another; some appear more thorny than others, yes, but they all lead to the same destination. Seeing the acrid smoke from the camp-fires of his one-time companions in the valley below, the Seeker appreciates the crisp, untainted air he now breathes. He begins to realise that he is free: free of his erroneous belief in the valueless wayside sign; and free of the futility and folly of the hatred, pettiness, conflict and back-stabbing of his fellow-man.

'The Seeker then looks in all directions. He sees the sky above and the earth below, both united on the horizon. He sees the rising sun casting its rays on heaven and earth alike. And when he looks below, he realises that there is the same unity in all things; the world below is whole; there are no conflicting parts, segments or divisions. Everything is *one*, and as he surveys the breathtaking grandeur of that total oneness he becomes *one* with it; he becomes *whole*. From this moment, he is not the Seeker any more. He is now a dweller in the realm of the True Self.'

Illusion

'Explain to me how the Ego-mind creates and maintains a world of illusion,' I said to both Guides.

After a few seconds of silence, the taller Guide spoke. 'The best way to explain this is to start by telling you a story. It is the story of a monkey. Not an ordinary monkey, but an Ego-monkey. The Ego-monkey lives in a fertile valley of unsurpassed beauty. It is densely populated with fruit trees. The fruit trees are not ordinary either: they bear fruit all year round.

'At dawn one morning, the Ego-monkey wakes up. He is in the branches of a fruit tree overlooking the valley. He has spent the night in this tree, and although he does not realise it, he has spent every night of his life in this tree. The tree, like all the others in the valley, bears fruit throughout the year, but this particular tree differs from the others. It is called a Destiny tree, and because it is a Destiny tree, it has a special relationship with, and a special power over, the Ego-monkey. Its power is inescapable; no matter where the Ego-monkey travels in the valley he is always brought back to this tree. And so, night after night, he reclines on a cluster of forked branches that jut out from the tree-trunk.

'The morning sun peeps above the horizon. The air is fresh; the birds are singing and calling to each other. The Ego-monkey stands and stretches his body. He inhales a lung-full of fresh air, then settles down to preen himself. By the time he has finished with his preening, he is wide awake. He is also bristling with self-importance.

'The Ego-monkey is hungry. He looks at the bunches of fruit that surround him in the tree, but the fruit that he sees has no appeal. He sees the same fruit in the valley, day after day; it looks uninteresting; not at all enticing or exotic. The Ego-monkey decides that this fruit is not for him. He is much too important to consume what he perceives to be ordinary fruit. He convinces himself that he deserves much better.

'So he leaves his tree and goes off in search of "better" fruit. His search takes him from one tree to another. He swings from one branch to the next, never climbing too high in any tree. After he has travelled through ten or twelve trees, he happens to look out through the branches of the tree he occupies. Far away in the distance, he sees a group of trees that appear different from the rest; they seem to shimmer with brightly-coloured, exotic fruit. The monkey's heart leaps with excitement. This is what he has been searching for all his life: trees filled with an abundance of "superior" fruit. And off he goes as fast as he can jump and swing, heading for the shimmering trees in the distance.

'The day wears on. The Ego-monkey is getting tired. Although each tree that he passes through is filled with fruit, he ignores them. He intends to gorge himself when he reaches the superior fruit in the distance.

'As afternoon approaches he pops his head out through a gap in the leaves to check his bearing. Much to his astonishment, he discovers that the shimmering trees are nowhere to be seen. He climbs higher and takes a good look in every direction, but all he sees is sameness. Every tree in the valley looks the same. The Ego-monkey becomes confused, agitated and annoyed. What, or who, has cheated him out of his exotic fruit?

'What the Ego-monkey did not realise is that the morning sunlight, slanting on the leaves of that particular group of trees, had made their shiny leaves look brighter. The Ego-monkey had mistakenly thought that the sunlight shimmering on the leaves was brightly-coloured pieces of fruit. What he had seen was an illusion.

'But the Ego-monkey is a stubborn monkey. He decides to carry on searching for better quality fruit. He convinces himself that there has to be a tree in the valley that bears the kind of fruit he desires. He also tells himself that he will never be happy until he gets what he wants.

'So he sets off in the same direction from which he has come. He travels all afternoon, and as evening approaches he finds a fruit tree that looks more appealing than anything he has seen all day. "At last," says the famished Ego-monkey, "I have found a fruit tree that provides me with the quality of fruit that I deserve." And without further analysis, the monkey promptly gorged himself on the fruit of this tree.

'Again, the Ego-monkey was fooled. He did not realise that the fruit tree in which he sat was the same tree he had started out from that morning. It was the Destiny tree. And that morning, he had condemned the fruit he now ate – it was not good enough for him at the time! After he ate his fill, the bone-weary Ego-monkey sat down and reflected on the events of the day. His mind contemplated the exotic fruit he had seen in the distance. His failure to acquire this "fruit" made him feel frustrated, dejected and depressed. The more he thought about his failure, the more depressed he became. Even when he should have been comfortably asleep, he worried and fretted about his failure.

'The next morning, at dawn, the Ego-monkey awakens to another day. He does not hear the bird-song; he does not smell the fresh air. His mind is cluttered by thoughts of what he has to do. The Ego-monkey has a tough day ahead of him. He is setting out to find the shimmering, exotic fruit.'

After giving the Guide's story some thought, I wondered if the Ego-monkey ever realised that he was chasing an illusion. If he did not, then he would waste his whole life searching for something that did not exist. I wondered if there were a way in which the Ego-monkey could extricate himself from this predicament.

'There is a way,' the Guide said. 'All the monkey has to do is climb high enough in his own tree, the tree of Destiny. When he climbs high enough, he will then be able to see the light of the morning sun. And through observation and contemplation, he will see the shimmering effect of the morning sunlight on the leaves of the trees in the distance. He will also notice that this effect disappears with the afternoon sun. At that point, he will come to realise that what he sees is nothing more than an illusion. Once he recognises the illusion, the reality of his own tree will become apparent, and he will no longer have to search outside his own tree for something to make him happy.

'The human Ego-mind and the Ego-monkey behave in much the same way. The lives of many individuals consist of one long procession of wants. Every day, from morning 'til night, the individual's life is devoted to servicing *wants*. The individual travels a treadmill, whereby the satisfaction of one want gives rise to another. As soon as one want is gratified, another takes its place to fill the void. Consider this carefully: Can peace of mind, harmony and happiness be found in the incessant pursuit of wants and desires? The answer is "no."

'The pursuit of wants and desires is a treadmill of illusion, daily struggles, anxieties and stress, where happiness and joy are as impermanent as fleeting shadows. The individual says, "If I get such and such I will be happy." But that happiness lasts only until the novelty of having such and such wears off; then the excitement and lustre leaves the individual's life. And when life becomes drab, dull and boring, the individual will want something else to brighten up his life. In this way clothing, personal items, furniture, fittings, electrical goods, cars and houses are being continually replaced, or traded in, for something "better." And what does this continual pursuit of "better" things do for the individual? In most cases, it brings added financial pressure and its attendant stress and agitation. And because of financial pressures, the individual will *want* more money, which may cause the individual to *want* a better job. And on, and on, it goes. One want leads to another until, in the end, the individual becomes enslaved by an habitual merry-go-round of daily *wants*.'

I contemplated what the Guide said, but I failed to see any solution to this situation. In our commercial world all things are manufactured and marketed expressly for people to want them. So how can a person escape this?

'If the individual so chooses, he can stop wanting. That is all it takes: stop wanting. Want is an illusion. Want is a habit. It is a mirage created and maintained by the Ego-mind. The Ego-mind will always want external things in order to prop up its own sense of existence and gratify itself into the bargain.

'As you know, wanting starts at an early age; look at how children always want things. This wanting will continue unceasingly throughout life, unless the individual puts a stop to it.'

'You make it sound like it's wrong to want,' I suggested.

'No. There is nothing inherently wrong in wanting. There are valid wants: the want to love and to be loved; the want of water, food, adequate clothing, money to survive, a comfortable home; education, books and reading material to learn from; the want of premises, tools and equipment to creatively utilize talents and skills; the want to belong to family and community; and the want to procreate. These wants are necessary to survival.

'There are also unnecessary wants: the want of one individual to change

121

another individual's point of view or behaviour; the want to be right all the time; the want to be better than others; the want to have more material things, and to have better quality material things than anybody else; the want to look better than others in the social group; the want to have power and control over others; the want to climb the social ladder; the want to win all the time; the want to gratify the Ego-self by cheating, stealing and exploiting others; the want of tobacco, alcohol, and narcotic drugs. And perhaps the most dispensable want of all is the want of wealth. Not money, but wealth. This particular want wastes more time in an individual's life than many of the other wants put together. The want of wealth is like the Ego-monkey chasing illusory fruit, day after day.'

I thought about this for a moment, then replied, 'But most people do not want wealth for wealth's sake. They want wealth because it will free them from their humdrum, often bleak, existences.'

'Yes,' the Guide answered, 'but will it set them free? That is the illusion. Wealth may free you from one set of circumstances, but it may well enslave you in another.'

The Guide fell silent, giving me the opportunity to think about what he had said. I asked what could be done to stop unnecessary wanting.

'The first step is contemplation. You must learn to think about your wants. You must learn to discern wants from needs. You must learn to differentiate between the essential and the unessential. When a want arises in your mind, ask yourself if you really need it. Write your want on paper – it may help you to study it thoughtfully. By recognizing and acknowledging the illusion of your want, your desire, you will stop wasting energy hankering after something that, in reality, you do not need. So look carefully at, and contemplate, your wants. You will find that most of them are illusions, they are not real needs.'

I tried to imagine what it would be like not to want, but my concept of this was unclear.

'If you wish to know what it is like to not want, then you should practice *non-doing*,' the Guide said.

'What is non-doing?' I inquired.

'It is *being*,' he answered. 'Non-doing is being.'

This conversation failed to make sense. I wondered if I, or the Guide, were having an "off" day.

The Guide explained. 'The way of humankind is to do. The average human being is constantly involved in doing; from morning 'til night it is do, do, do. The question on the lips of most individuals is, "What are we going to do today?" Doing keeps the Ego intact. "I am painting a house", "I am playing tennis", "I am watching TV." Do you see how doing reinforces the "I"?

'On the other hand, non-doing diminishes the "I." While you are engaged in non-doing the "I" has nothing to relate to; it cannot say, "I am doing this", or "I am doing that." In a state of non-doing the "I" is doing nothing. Non-doing is *being*. In a state of non-doing the individual just *is,* and there are no wants. Want is annihilated. So to know what it is like not to want, you must practice non-doing.

'Select a day when you have no engagements. Unplug your telephone and put a "Do Not Disturb" sign on your door. Set yourself up in one room. Put a comfortable armchair by the window where you will sit throughout the day. Bring fruit and water to eat and drink. Remember, you are going to spend the whole day alone with yourself: no radio; no television; no noise of any description; and no newspapers, magazines, books or other reading material. When you step into the room on the morning of this day, you will leave behind all thoughts of commitments, responsibilities, habits, wants and all the things that anchor your mind to the external world.

'Be prepared to leave outside your cigarettes, tea or coffee; do not bring your habits into the room. Enter the room and sit in your armchair. Breathe deeply and relax. Gaze at the sky through your window. It does not matter if the sky is blue or grey; simply gaze at it. Observe it. Do not allow your mind to drift backward or forward in time. Be constantly aware of the present. Be aware of your feet resting on the floor, and the chair you are sitting on. Do not allow yourself to daydream. If you begin to feel uneasy, change your point of visual focus or engage in listening to the sound of your breath as you inhale and exhale.

'Be aware of yourself as an observer, and, at the same time, be aware of the observed. Do not form concepts or opinions about what you are observing or listening to. Simply allow your mind to rest on the sight of the sky or the sound of your breathing.

'By practising non-doing once a week, you will begin to realise what it feels like to not want. And by learning the art of not wanting, you are learning how to be free.'

'You once talked about non-productive activity,' I said to the Guide. 'To me the practice of non-doing sounds very much like non-productive activity.'

'This is not so,' he replied. 'The practice of non-doing is productive on an inner level. Continual practice not only releases you from habitual wants, but also expands your field of consciousness. The only way to know this is to practice it.'

Freedom

'Freedom is a state of mind; nothing more, nothing less. A man bound hand and foot inside a prison fortress can be as free as the wind if he so chooses. All he has to do is forget his physical situation and allow his consciousness to merge with the Limitless – the Infinite. But as long as a thought remains in his Ego-mind, he will not attain this freedom. If his Ego-mind tells him that he is bound hand and foot inside a prison, then that thought makes him a prisoner. If he desires to physically escape, then that desire will make his bonds feel tighter. But if all thoughts of imprisonment are wiped from his mind, if his mind is empty, if his mind is free, how can he be a prisoner?

'If an individual is poor and he constantly reminds himself of his poverty, then he will become imprisoned in poverty. If an individual suffers ill health and constantly complains about his illness, then that individual will become a prisoner of illness. If an individual falls prey to unhappiness and bemoans that state of unhappiness, unhappiness will grasp the individual's heart and keep it under lock and key. If an individual becomes the victim of an addiction and has an unceasing desire to satisfy that addiction, then that desire will build a wall around the individual and confine him to the addiction. An individual who is being abused in the home will say that he or she cannot leave the abuser because of fear, guilt or remorse that may be experienced afterwards, but it is these feelings that keep the individual trapped in the undesirable situation.

'At the beginning, I said that freedom is a state of mind. That is a truth. But freedom is also an empty mind. Living in an empty state of mind is not the Western way. In your fast-paced world the Ego-mind has developed its own way of life. It has now reached a point where, during waking hours, it never stops thinking, imagining, daydreaming or fantasizing about the things it wants. As a result, the average individual never stops wanting; never stops doing; never stops seeking excitement, novelty and sensory gratification. And while involved in all these things, how can the individual be free?

'And what has all this fast-paced thinking and doing achieved for the individual? There is more stress-related illness in your world than ever before. Dependency on alcohol, prescribed and illegal drugs increases all the time.'

I had a mental image of people hustling and bustling along a busy, city street. Cars were jammed on the street, impatiently honking at each other. Buses zoomed along bus lanes, spewing black diesel fumes at the hurrying pedestrians. It all looked so natural, so necessary. I tried to imagine everything and everyone standing still, but could not. It came to mind that life without activity would be a very boring, stagnant affair. I conveyed this thought to the Guide.

'There is doing, and there is doing,' he commented. There is doing which is necessary, and doing which is not necessary. The modern Ego-mind has reached a point where it cannot tell the necessary from the unnecessary. It is too overloaded and preoccupied with external things.'

'What is the difference between necessary doing and unnecessary doing?' I inquired.

'Only the individual can know what is necessary or unnecessary in his life. The trick is to empty the mind sufficiently, so that you can tell one from the other. Using your own case as an example, necessary doing is researching, learning and writing. That is the natural order in your life. If you deviate from that and spend all the day in non-productive activity, then you have engaged in unnecessary doing.'

'Can you give me an example of "non-productive activity"?' I asked.

'Yes. Non-productive activity is activity that is aimless – purposeless – like sitting around for hours on end, talking with people for the sake of talking; dwelling on things that have happened in the recent or distant past; allowing your mind to project onto something that may, or may not, happen in the future; or taking an inordinate interest in the behaviour of others. These are some of the most common examples of unnecessary doing. They entrap the mind and waste time and energy. Also, aimless thoughts and conversation often lead to discordant emotions, which in turn consume even more energy.

'Life is meant to flow. As you were told by one of our colleagues: "Life should flow calmly and gracefully, like an abundant stream." And like a stream, the daily activity of life should flow within a prescribed channel. When you are involved in necessary doing, you are like the stream following its natural course, and the stream that follows its natural course is always free. But when you become engaged in unnecessary doing, your energy becomes diverted from its natural flow. What would happen to a stream whose water diverged into smaller channels along its route? Eventually, the stream would no longer be a stream. It would no longer be *its true self*.'

Reality

'In your world, what humankind call reality in not true reality. It is perceived reality, or perceptional reality, if you wish to call it that. Perceptional reality is an individual's comprehension of the world as he or she sees it. Each individual's comprehension of the world is based, in the first instance, on information received from the five physical senses. These are sensory perceptions; they enter the field of Ego-consciousness where they are interpreted, and evaluated, according to the individual's mental and emotional conditioning. In this process, a particular sensory perception will end up being accepted or rejected, or end up being slanted in a way that is compatible with the attitude of the Ego.

'Let us first take a look at how the Ego can accept or reject a perception. Supposing you look out of your window right now, and you see a person hovering in mid-air. Instantly, your Ego consciousness will tell you that what you are seeing is impossible; that what you are perceiving is not real. Yet, the phenomenon of levitation exists; it is real. You have read convincing accounts of levitation; you have seen the levitation of an electric heater with your own eyes; therefore, on an intellectual level you accept the idea of levitation. But if you were to see a person levitating outside your window, your Ego would now react differently. You would not say to yourself: "Oh look, there is someone levitating outside my window. It looks like fun." No, your Ego would not react like that. Because you have never seen a human being levitating, your Ego will either dismiss the phenomenon entirely, or it will become so shocked and confused that it will refuse to offer any critical evaluation whatsoever. In short, the Ego will not believe what you see with your eyes, until it is coerced into doing so by way of rational explanation.'

The Guide's example of a person levitating in the back garden caused my mind to wander. I thought of how people would react if I told them that I had seen a person floating in mid-air! This thought proved how difficult it would be for the Ego to accept the concept of levitation.

The Guide interrupted my thoughts. 'Now we will deal with how perceptions can become slanted by the Ego. At one time, you read of four individuals who had witnessed an accident from the same viewpoint. Each saw the same accident; yet when each individual gave an account of what they saw, each account was somewhat different than that of the others. Each individual perceived the facts of the accident according to the conditioning and attitude of their own respective Ego-minds. They had witnessed the same event in four different ways.

'As this example demonstrates, there are as many so-called realities as there are individuals on your planet. We see that perceived reality means different things to different people. For instance, the reality perceived by a seventeenth-century soothsayer would be much different from that of a modern-day sports-star. So, too, the reality of an individual on Skid Row would be much different from the sense of reality experienced by a successful entrepreneur. As an exercise, imagine what these two different realities might be like. Try to see in your mind's eye, and feel within yourself, what a homeless individual's perception of reality might be, and likewise the entrepreneur's. Try to understand what so-called reality would feel like for both of these individuals. Once you reach this understanding, you will discover how distinctly dissimilar perceived realities can be.

'Another example worth noting lies in how individuals perceive each other. Individuals perceive and describe other people in positive or negative terms; mainly in terms of "good" and "bad." If another person acts in a way that pleases the individual – by giving something to the individual, or by doing something for the individual – then the individual will invariably proclaim that person to be "good." On the other hand, if that person acts in a way that displeases the individual, then that person is classed as "bad." Quite often, when a another person acts in neither one way nor the other, the individual will refer to him or her as "no good." This is because the other person, in the eyes of the individual, has failed to contribute something towards the individual's mental, emotional or physical welfare. From a True Reality point of view, "the other person" in this example is neither "good" nor "bad" in the critical sense. He or she is simply perceived that way by the individual's Ego.

'And the individual's perception of a person can change from one day to the next, one hour to the next, or from one mood to the next, depending on the actions of the other person and the mood of the individual. Are you now beginning to see how defective and flawed perceptional reality really is? It is this defective and flawed mode of perceiving that drives your world. Your world is constructed of, constructed on, and maintained by masses of defective and flawed perceptions. Does it surprise you to know that Buddhists refer to this world as the "world of illusion"?'

'Why is the human perception of reality so flawed?' I asked.

'Firstly, it is because the human physical senses are primarily equipped to perceive only the surface of things. Secondly, perceptions become adulterated by the individual's mental and emotional states – by the attitude of the Ego at the time of perception.

'The greatest flaw in the process of human perception is the unshakeable reliance on the physical senses. This is what limits and distorts perceived reality most of all. The physical senses can only see the surface, the appearance of things. You have heard the adage: "Never judge a book by its cover." This piece of advice applies to what I am saying. The physical senses cannot penetrate, or see, past the surface of anything. And in order to know and understand True Reality, it is necessary to get past the surface, the appearance of things. As in judging the proverbial book, it is necessary to discover what lies inside the cover.'

The Guide fell silent, as if waiting for a question.

'Can you give an example of what you mean by the "appearance," the "surface of things"?' I asked.

'Yes,' he answered, without pausing for further thought. 'Supposing an individual asks you to go to a certain house and bring back a detailed account of what that home is like. Note that the individual uses the word "home."

'The home you are asked to examine is a single-storey town house, situated about twenty metres from the street. The house, with its front lawn and flower garden, is hidden from the street by a high hedge. Effectively, the entire front cannot be seen from the street, except through two narrow gateways. These gateways lead to opposite ends of the house, north and south. A trellis of rose bushes runs from the hedge to the front door of the house, dividing the front lawn and garden into two areas.

'Looking through the north gate, only half of the house can be seen because of the rose trellis. From this angle you see a patch of untidy lawn bordered with weed-filled flower beds. You can see rubble and various bits of building materials, thrown untidily on the walkway by the gable end of the house. The view is unpleasant. If you were unaware of the existence of another gateway to the house, you would look no further and accept what you saw. Your report on the state of this house would be anything but complimentary.

'But supposing you look through the other gate, the one at the south end of the house. The view from this perspective is much different. At this end, the lawn is trimmed neatly and tidily; there are flower beds in full bloom. Adorning the gable end of the house are hanging baskets suspended from wrought iron brackets and filled with blooming flowers of various genus and colour. Beyond the gable end, at the rear of the house, you can see a lush palm tree overlooking a slice of manicured grass. In general, you are quite impressed by the tidiness and the relative beauty of what you see.

'Now you have viewed the house from two different angles. From a perceptional point of view, you saw the so-called reality of the house in two different ways. The reality of your view from the north gate was that the house was untidy and not very pleasing to the eye. Your view from the south gate apprised you of a quaint beauty surrounding the house. Your perceived reality and your ultimate evaluation depend on which gate you look through.

'But, let us not lose sight of your task. The individual requested a detailed description of this particular home. Up until now you have merely looked at the surface, the facade, the appearance, the superficial reality. Apart from the superficial, perceptional reality, which confusingly presented itself in two different ways, you have not seen the inside of the house. Until you are able to go through the gates and gain access to the interior of the building, you will never know the completeness of the stranger's home. If you cannot get inside, you can never tell the individual what it feels like to ramble through the house from room to room. You will never be able to describe the welcoming smells of cooked food, furniture polish, a particular scent of air freshener, or the crisp smell of fresh bed linen. You will not know how the furniture looks, or what it feels like to touch or sit on. You will not know the kind of cutlery and crockery the house contains. It is all these things that give the house its completeness and its feeling of home. Not only that, but the entire house and each of its contents also have their own energy fields, their own unique energy frequencies. It is these combined energy fields that give the house its atmosphere, its ambience, its aura; in other words, its essence.

'This is the closest I can get to explaining the nature of True Reality. True Reality is the essence, the energy, that works through and sustains all things. It is this essence that gives everything its *completeness*. Even non-organic matter has its own essence. It has its own particular energy frequency and configuration, and it depends upon that frequency and configuration to maintain its existence as a particular thing. For example, if someone dramatically altered the energy configuration [atomic structure] of a piece of rock, the rock would no longer be the exact same piece of rock.

'But that is another subject. Let us finish our communication by saying that True Reality is the essence, the energy, the completeness of all things. Since this energy is an inseparable part of the Cosmos – the whole, True Reality is like the *whole*; it is all embracing; it is *one*. It cannot be anything more: it cannot be anything less.

Truth v. Non-Truth

'The world you perceive through the Ego is a world of duality; a world of opposites; a world of light and dark, hot and cold, positive and negative. It is a world of degrees and extremes; a world of double standards, where that which appears to be real is not real. Nothing is as it appears to be. In this materialistic world of yours, Truth is buried deep; so deep, that many fail to find it in an entire lifetime. Because Truth is so cleverly concealed, non-truth reigns supreme. Non-truth occupies the throne of Truth, and in this position of power, non-truth receives the adulation that rightfully belongs to Truth. To put it another way, in your modern, commercial world, the masses have accepted, and live by, rules and ideas that have no basis in Truth.

'Therefore, everything that is perceived to be of great importance, and all that people revere, and all the material things that people strive for are like elusive shadows on a wall. Shadows on a wall cast by candlelight rely on the candle flame for their existence, and the candle flame relies on circumstances around it for its existence. If a strong draught buffeted the candle flame, it would splutter and cease to be. And when the light from the candle flame ceases to be, the shadows also cease to be. They are no longer shadows; therefore, they have no enduring substance. So it is with all the material things of the world.'

It sounded like the Guide, in an abstract way, was referring to the physical body and physical death. I asked if this were the case.

'Yes, that is one meaning, but there is another. In times of serious physical illness, in times of emotional despair, in times of grief and in times of mental depression, that which is important to the individual ceases to be important. Personal possessions lose their perceived value. Personal ambition loses its power. Anxiety about personal appearance, prestige, social interaction and all those other things that normally occupy Ego-consciousness fade into the background. They are no longer important. They are like shadows on a wall. The light goes out and the shadows cease to be. Therefore, all these external things that daily imprison the Ego-consciousness of the individual have no substance. The only substance that they can ever have is that which is given to them by the individual. They have no basis in reality; they have no basis in Universal Truth.

'Let us examine the meaning of Truth. Truth is universal; it has no boundaries. It does not change from one country to the next, from one culture to the next, or from one century to the next. It is constant. It just is. An example of Universal Truth is to be found in the fifth Commandment: "Thou shalt not kill." As you can see, this Commandment serves the best interest of all living things, equally and unequivocally. This is the basis of Truth. In order for anything to call itself "Truth" it must apply to, and serve, the best interests of all living things, equally and unequivocally. Because of its integrity, justice and purity, Truth is the closest you will get to the Word of God. Truth is rooted in, and originates in, the realm of Spirit.'

'There is room for Truth in everything. Truth can be embodied in contemplation; in belief; in a statement; in an opinion, an intent, a principle or premise; in action or a series of actions; or in rules or laws. But where Truth is needed most of all is within systems, be it a religious system or a social system. It is crucial that all systems have their foundations in, and be constructed with, the building blocks of Truth.'

Again the Guide fell silent. It gave me the opportunity to reflect on his last statements. I began to think along the lines that if something is not true then it must be a lie.

'Not exactly,' he answered. 'A lie, as you understand it, is a statement that has no basis in fact; a statement that is fabricated. The opposite of Truth is different. We refer to it as "non-truth." A non-truth is not easily detectable. Not in the same way as a barefaced lie. In your society today, non-truths are generally accepted as Truths.

'Again, the fault lies within the Ego-mind. It tends to taint, or colour, everything it produces. Invariably, its own mental and emotional attitudes unconsciously creep into the production process. Whatever passes through Ego-consciousness ends up being slanted in a particular way. In other words, if an individual sets out to devise a set of rules or a particular system, he will do so from the point of view of his personal likes and dislikes. This is what I mean by Truth being coloured by the Ego.

'And when a Truth is influenced by the Ego-mind it becomes tarnished with self-interest; it becomes self-serving; it becomes a non-truth. Therefore, a non-truth is anything that serves the best interests of the few at the expense of the many.'

After giving this particular discussion some thought, I brought up the subject again the following day.

'I've been thinking about what you said yesterday regarding Truth,' I said to the Guide. 'You said that it is crucial for systems be built on Truth. Could you give me an example of Truth in this instance.'

I expected the Guide to think about his answer, as he often did before he spoke. But his answer was delivered so swiftly, that I was not mentally prepared for it. I had to focus hard to keep pace with his communication.

'There are three basic Truths that will serve the whole of humankind and the entire planet.

1. Do not harm, or endanger, the well-being of yourself in any way, or by any means.

2. Do not harm, or endanger, the well-being of another human in any way, or by any means.

3.   Do not harm, or endanger, the well-being of any living thing, including the planet, Earth, in any way, or by any means.'

Epilogue

In thinking back over the past eighteen years, I realise that there has been a considerable shift in my way of thinking, especially in the past eleven months. All the grasping and all the clinging to false notions and emotions have dissolved. There was a time when I looked at situations, I would see only the aspect of the situation that suited my own feelings and needs. Now I can look at situations in their entirety, consider all aspects, good and bad, and not react emotionally, one way or the other. I have found that much of what I held important throughout my life was not important at all: it was an illusion.

Today, in thinking about my perceived progress, I decided to consult the Guides to get their views on this matter. I expected them to say that I had progressed greatly. But they did not.

'You have scarcely scratched the surface,' the taller Guide said. 'Your progress up until now has been erratic. It has been a series of stops and starts. Yet, it worked. If you really want to make progress, you must apply yourself in a systematic and disciplined manner. You are like a man who wants to swim but is afraid; each time you dip your toes in the water, you quickly pull them out again. At this stage of your spiritual development, you must forget about whether or not the water is too cold or too deep. You have to dive off the edge. There is no other way.'

'What do you mean by "diving off the edge"?' I asked.

'You must throw yourself whole-heartedly into the *idea* of progress and development. Immerse yourself in the power of that idea; feel the idea. When you can feel the idea, its power will carry you along effortlessly.'

I did not understand what the Guide was telling me. How could anyone "feel" an idea?

'How would you feel if you won a new motor car?' asked the Guide. 'Think of how you would feel.'

I thought about this. The idea had appeal. It felt exciting.

'There you are,' he said. 'You *felt* the idea of winning a car. It is the same with spiritual development: you must feel the idea of what you want to achieve. That is the first step.

'The next step is to purify your system. This is achieved by cleansing diets and realistic periods of fasting. Avoid meat, avoid cigarettes, avoid alcohol, avoid chemically treated water and food. These things densify and distort the energy system.

'Exercise your body. Spend three hours a day exercising. Give at least half-an-hour of this time to Yoga practice.

'Meditate regularly. Spent quality time in the realm of the True Self. Incorporate periods of prayer. If you are consistent in your efforts, your energy system will become increasingly refined.'

'And what will happen then?' I asked.

'You will be ready to project your consciousness into the higher astral realms,' he answered. 'As I said, you have scarcely scratched the surface. There are worlds of great beauty to be explored once your energy system is proportionately refined.

'And refining your energy system will not only open doorways to the higher worlds, but it will open another doorway in your own world. It will give you the power to heal.'

Although, for the past few years, I had a mild interest in healing, I was surprised by the Guide's last remark.

'How will that happen?' I enquired. 'How will I get the power to heal?'

'When your system becomes spiritually attuned, spiritual power will be able to flow through you. It cannot do so at the moment because your own system is not properly cleansed and balanced. But if you follow our recommendations, you can become a healer. When the time is right, we will show you how.'

'But am I not supposed to write in this life?' I asked.

'Yes. You can write, and you can also heal. What is to stop you from balancing your life between both? In order to research and write about the higher planes, it will be necessary to live your life as I have just suggested. Living the way of the Spirit automatically opens the door to spiritual power. It is something that happens naturally. And once you have access to spiritual power, why not use it to relieve human suffering?'

What he said made sense. My train of thought drifted onto healing; I was trying to remember healing methods I had read about. The Guide interrupted my thoughts.

'You must work hard on refining your energy system. This will require more discipline than you now realise. If, and when, you reach the required state, then we will discuss the matter of how.

'But the choice is yours,' he continued. 'Bear in mind, once you make the decision, there is no going back. Life, as you know it, will never be the same again. You will have to say "good-bye" to your old self, your old ways, your old world. If you do decide to move forward, your consciousness will spend as much time in the astral worlds as it will in this one. In other words, it will be necessary to balance your time between two worlds: the world of Spirit, and the world of matter.

'If you decide to move forward, your life-span on the earth will be considerably lengthened; you may live another forty-five years. If you discipline yourself as we have advised, and, if you continue to learn, you may be able to free yourself from the earthly life, death and rebirth cycle. When this existence is at an end, you may become a Teacher on our plane, and help others as we have helped you.

'On the other hand, if you decide to remain at the level you are at, your life on this plane will not be as long as you would like it to be. And, you may have to return here [earth], in another existence, to complete your learning.

'We have now shown you where you are at. There is little more we can do for you until you have made your decision.'

The Guide fell silent. I felt our meeting was at an end. I was about to say that I had almost finished this book, when the shorter guide said, 'Every beginning is an end, and every end is a beginning.'

In light of what I learned today, and in light of the Guide's last statement, it looks as if my *spiritual journey* is just beginning.

Bibliography

Balcombe, B F, *As I See It, A Psychics Guide to Developing your Sensing and Healing Abilities*, London, Judy Piatkus.

Brennan, J H, *Astral Doorways*, Wellingborough, Northamptonshire, Thorsons.

Bruyere, R L, *Chakra Healing* (Cassette and Booklet), New York, Distributed by St. Martin's Press.

Gill, P, *The Way of a Healer*, Dublin, The Mercier Press.

Le Shan, L, *Clairvoyant Reality – Towards a General Theory of the Paranormal*, Wellingborough, Northamptonshire, Turnstone Press Ltd.

Monroe, R A, *Journeys out of the Body*, London, Souvenir Press Ltd.

Rinpoche, S, *The Tibetan Book of Living and Dying*, London, Random House UK Ltd.

Russell, P, *The TM Technique*, London, Arkana.

Sherwood, K, *Chakra Therapy, For Personal Growth and Healing*, St. Paul, Minnesota, Llewellyn Publications.

Suzuki, S, *Zen Mind, Beginner's Mind*, New York & Tokyo, Weatherhill.

Twitchell, P, *Eckankar*, San Diego, California, Illuminated Way Press.